Lecture Notes of the Institute for Computer Sciences, Social Informatics and Telecommunications Engineering 256

More information about this series at http://www.springer.com/series/8197

Al-Sakib Khan Pathan · Zubair Md. Fadlullah
Mohamed Guerroumi (Eds.)

Smart Grid and Internet of Things

Second EAI International Conference, SGIoT 2018
Niagara Falls, ON, Canada, July 11, 2018
Proceedings

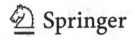

Springer

Editors
Al-Sakib Khan Pathan
Southeast University
Dhaka, Bangladesh

Zubair Md. Fadlullah
Tohoku University
Sendai, Miyagi, Japan

Mohamed Guerroumi
University of Science and Technology
Houari Boumediene
Bab Ezzouar, Algeria

ISSN 1867-8211 ISSN 1867-822X (electronic)
Lecture Notes of the Institute for Computer Sciences, Social Informatics
and Telecommunications Engineering
ISBN 978-3-030-05927-9 ISBN 978-3-030-05928-6 (eBook)
https://doi.org/10.1007/978-3-030-05928-6

Library of Congress Control Number: 2018964131

This Springer imprint is published by the registered company Springer Nature Switzerland AG
The registered company address is: Gewerbestrasse 11, 6330 Cham, Switzerland

Preface

We are very delighted to introduce the proceedings of the second edition of 2018 European Alliance for Innovation (EAI) International Conference on Smart Grid and Internet of Things (SGIoT). This conference has attracted and brought together researchers, developers, and practitioners from different parts of the globe, who are currently exerting their efforts in developing smart grid and IoT technologies.

The technical program of SGIoT 2018 consisted of 14 full papers, including one invited paper in oral presentation sessions in the main conference track and one workshop on Applications and Technologies in Big Data (ATBD 2018). In addition to the high-quality technical paper presentations, the technical program also featured two keynote speeches. The invited speakers for the keynote speeches were Dr. Salama Ikki from Lakehead University, Thunder Bay, Ontario, Canada, and Dr. Andriy Miranskyy from Ryerson University, Ontario, Canada. The ATBD workshop in the conference aimed to address various aspects of techniques and applications in big data research and provide a forum for the presentation and discussion of innovative ideas, research results, applications, and experience from around the globe as well as highlight activities in the related areas.

Coordination among the steering chair, Imrich Chlamtac, and the steering members, Al-Sakib Khan Pathan, Zubair Md. Fadlullah, and Salimur Choudhury, was essential for the success of the conference. It was also a great pleasure to work with such an excellent organizing team, all of who did their parts in organizing and supporting the conference. In particular, the contribution of the Technical Program Committee members, led by the TPC chairs, Dr. Salimur Choudhury and Dr. Akramul Azim, eased the paper review and selection process and also helped in preparing the program schedule. We sincerely appreciate all the key members' sincere support. Last but not the least, we are also very grateful to the Conference Manager, Radka Pincakova, for her constant support and all the authors who submitted their papers to SGIoT 2018 and traveled a long distance to present their papers.

We strongly believe that the SGIoT conference provides a good platform for all researchers, students, developers, and practitioners to discuss all scientific and technological aspects relevant to smart grid and IoT. We also expect that future SGIoT conferences will be as successful and stimulating as indicated by the contributions presented in this volume.

Al-Sakib Khan Pathan
Zubair Md. Fadlullah
Mohamed Guerroumi

Organization

Steering Committee

Chair

Imrich Chlamtac	Bruno Kessler Professor, University of Trento, Italy

Members

Al-Sakib Khan Pathan	Southeast University, Bangladesh
Salimur Choudhury	Lakehead University, Thunder Bay, Ontario, Canada
Zubair Md. Fadlullah	Tohoku University, Japan

Organizing Committee

General Co-chairs

Al-Sakib Khan Pathan	Southeast University, Bangladesh
Zubair Md. Fadlullah	Tohoku University, Japan

TPC Chair and Co-chair

Salimur Choudhury	Lakehead University, Thunder Bay, Ontario, Canada
Akramul Azim	University of Ontario Institute of Technology, Canada

Sponsorship and Exhibit Chair

Homero Toral Cruz	University of Quintana Roo, Mexico

Local Chair

Salimur Choudhury	Lakehead University, Thunder Bay, Ontario, Canada

Workshops Co-chairs

Md. Zakirul Alam Bhuiyan	Fordham University, USA
Mostafa Fouda	Benha University, Egypt

Publicity and Social Media Chair

Mubashir Husain Rehmani	COMSATS Institute of Information Technology, Wah Cantt, Pakistan

Publications Chair

Mohamed Guerroumi	University of Science and Technology Houari Boumediene, Algeria

Web Chair

Rasib Khan	Northern Kentucky University, USA

Posters and PhD Track Chair

Nurilla Avazov	Inha University, South Korea

Technical Program Committee

Iftekhar Ahmad	Edith Cowan University, Australia
Shawkat Ali	The University of Fiji, Lautoka, Fiji
AbdulRahman Alsamman	University of New Orleans, USA
Farrokh Aminifar	University of Tehran, Iran
Vijayan K. Asari	University of Dayton, USA
Md. Atiqur Rahman Ahad	Dhaka University, Bangladesh
Paolo Bellavista	University of Bologna, Italy
Josu Bilbao	IK4-IKERLAN, Spain
John Canning	University of Technology Sydney (UTS), Australia
Abdelouahid Ahmed Derhab	King Saud University, Saudi Arabia
Khalid Elgazzar	Carnegie Mellon University, USA
Omar Farooq	Aligarh Muslim University, India
Lim Tiong Hoo	Universiti Teknologi Brunei, Brunei
Muhammad Khurram Khan	King Saud University, Saudi Arabia
Qurban Ali Memon	UAE University, Al-Ain, UAE
Tamer M. Nadeem	Virginia Commonweath University, USA
M. A. Rashid	Massey University Albany, New Zealand
Abdur Razzaque	Dhaka University, Bangladesh
Shariful Shaikot	Microsoft, USA
Mohiuddin Ahmed	Canberra Institute of Technology, Australia
Shafiullah Khan	Kohat University of Science and Technology, Pakistan
Hae Young Lee	DuDu IT, South Korea
Karan Singh	Jawaharlal Nehru University, India
Junaid Chaudhry	Security Research Institute, Edith Cowan University, Australia
Sabu M. Thampi	Indian Institute of Information Technology and Management – Kerala, India
Houssem Mansouri	University of Ferhat Abbas Setif1, Algeria
Sofiane Hamrioui	University of Nantes, France
Yousaf Bin Zikria	Yeungnam University, South Korea
Amjad Anvari-Moghaddam	Aalborg University, Denmark
M. M. Hafizur Rahman	King Faisal University, Saudi Arabia
Zahoor Khan	Higher Colleges of Technology, UAE
Chen Chen	Argonne National Laboratory, USA
Mohamed Sellami	ISEP, France
Ali Balador	Mälardalen University, Sweden

Contents

Smart Grid and Internet of Things

Applications and Technologies

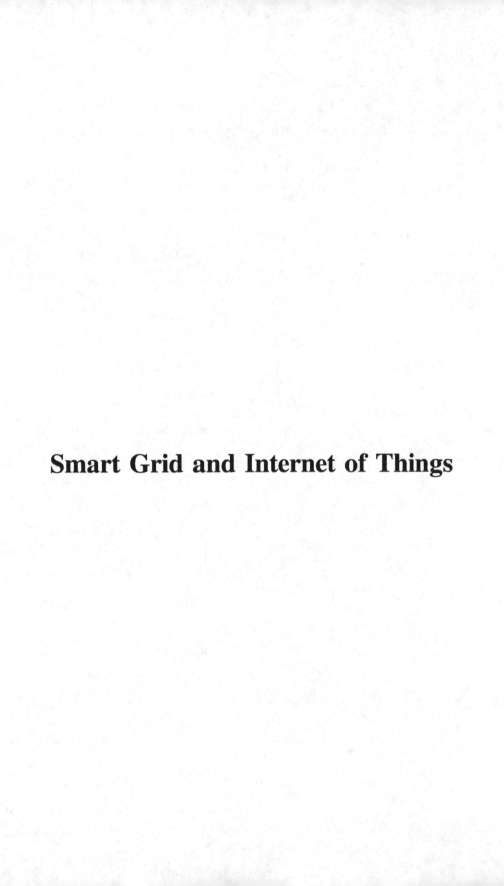

Smart Grid and Internet of Things

An Implementation of Harmonizing Internet of Things (IoT) in Cloud

Md. Motaharul Islam[1,2](✉), Zaheer Khan[3], and Yazed Alsaawy[2]

[1] Department of Computer Science and Engineering, BRAC University, Dhaka, Bangladesh
motaharul.islam@bracu.ac.bd

[2] Islamic University of Madinah AlMadinah, Medina, Kingdom of Saudi Arabia
yalsaawy@iu.edu.sa

[3] Khana-e-Noor University, Pole Mahmood Khan Shash Darak kabul, Kabul, Afghanistan
zaheeriut13@gmail.com

Abstract. With the evolution of Internet of Things (IoT), everything is going to be connected to the Internet and the data produced by IoT, will be used for different purposes. Since IoT generates huge amount of data, we need some scalable storage to store and compute the data sensed from the sensors. To overcome this issue, we need the integration of cloud and IoT so that the data might be stored and computed in a scalable environment. Harmonization of IoT in Cloud might be a novel solution in this regard. IoT devices will interact with each other using Constrained Application Protocol (CoAP). All the IoT devices will be assigned IP addresses for unique identification. In this paper, we have implemented harmonizing IoT in Cloud. We have used CoAP to get things connected to each other through the Internet. For the implementation we have used two sensors, fire detector and the sensor attached with the door which is responsible for opening the door. Thus the proposed implementation will be storing and retrieving the sensed data from the cloud. We have also compared our implementation with different parameters. The comparison shows that our implementation significantly improves the performance compared to the existing system.

Keywords: Harmonization · Cloud · Internet of Things
Constrained application protocol · Smart environment · Arduino shield

1 Introduction

Nowadays everything is getting smarter. With the evolution of the Internet of Things (IoT), the demand for users to use smart things are increased. In order to make things and environment smarter and connected the researchers are thinking to assign IP addresses [1] to all the smart devices [2]. These devices will have the capabilities of sensing and actuating the environment. Since huge amount of

A.-S. K. Pathan et al. (Eds.): SGIoT 2018, LNICST 256, pp. 3–12, 2019.
https://doi.org/10.1007/978-3-030-05928-6_1

data is sensed by the sensor from the smart environment we have to store and process it for further data analytics. To store the data cloud storage is a very good and reliable alternative.

Data from sensed environment would be transferred to the storage through Hypertext Transfer Protocol (HTTP) which is designed for the Internet devices. It consumes more time in case of GET and POST method. In this connection, a novel framework has been suggested to cooperate cloud-level IoT services on a smart device with the concept of Intention [3]. Captured data from sensors were stored in local machines. A repository might be used for storing the status of the sensors. The sensed data might be stored in the cloud using HTTP if required. In this paper concept of local repository is eliminated. A cloud based architecture is proposed where data will be stored in the cloud. Using cloud storage instead of physical storage will make it more reliable. If the data is stored in the cloud the aspect of physical damages and security will be enhanced as well. Internet and some gateways [4] might be used to connect the sensors to the cloud for storing and retrieving the required information. In order to provide the connection between the sensors some well-known protocols might be used.

For sensor-based connections two protocols are preferable Message Queue Telemetry Transport (MQTT) and Constrained Application Protocol (CoAP). In this paper we have introduced CoAP for the connectivity purpose instead of using HTTP. Using CoAP protocol in the connectivity area will make the system faster. On the other hand, CoAP protocol is designed for resource constraint smart devices where HTTP was designed for the traditional internet devices. In this paper CoAP is used to harmonize sensors with cloud in such a way that data taken from one of the sensor is a command towards next sensor in order to make an alert for smart doors in smart environment. Harmonization is the process of joining more than one devices to perform a single task. Harmonizing means that input is applied from different sources and output is combined by a group of sensors. Here, we harmonize two sensors to perform the task of alerting the doors if fire exists.

In the harmonization process cloud acts as a remote storage and IoT devices (e.g. sensors) act as actuators in the smart environment. The sensed data is collected from the environment and transferred to the cloud through CoAP in order to update the status of the sensors in the cloud. In this paper smart doors' sensors checks its' status in the cloud. If the status's value is above the defined threshold. Smart doors will be opened automatically for the fire exit. Two types of sensors will be used to control this scenario, smoke sensors and the sensors attached with the smart doors. The smoke sensor will be responsible to detect the existence of fire. If fire exists, it will send the sensed value to the cloud storage. In the storage the sensor will have a status and the value of its status will be initialized to the standard value. This value indicates that the temperature up to this threshold will be normal. If the sensed value passed to the storage is greater than defined threshold value then the status will be updated to that sensed value. The sensor attached with the door continuously checks the status of the smoke detector sensor. If it figures out that the status value is greater than defined threshold value, the door sensor will alert the door to be opened urgently.

Since the smart doors are opened automatically it may affect the security of the building. To ensure the security sensors may be placed inside the building and more specifically inside the room so the smart doors are controlled by the sensors inside the room. No sensor outside the building will be able to control the door.

The main contributions of this paper are as follows:

- We have proposed cloud based architecture for harmonizing IoT.
- We have implemented the architecture using CoAP.
- We have analyzed and compared our implementation with HTTP using different cloud platforms.
- We have compared CoAP with MQTT and have shown the suitability of CoAP over MQTT considering some text comparisons.
- We have compared CoAP with HTTP and the comparison shows that by using CoAP, performance has been increased by 33.76% and 11.45%, 10.83% and 19.98%, 10.52% and 16.92% using GET and POST methods respectively for Google cloud, Thingspeak and 000Webhost.

The rest of the paper is organized as follows. Section 2 reviews related works. System architecture is presented in Sect. 3. Section 4 describes algorithmic analysis. Section 5 represents the layered architecture of the proposed system. Section 6 shows the way of implementation. Section 7 shows the experimental evaluation. Finally Sect. 8 concludes the paper.

2 Related Works

Seung Woo Kum et. al. proposed IoT device delegate system [3]. This IoT device delegate has a database to store the information of devices. Device delegate creates data channel from the devices so that data can be streamed. An Intention Manager is also proposed. It makes decision for which action will be performed based on request from the devices. For acquiring data via data channel, they have used HTTP.

IoT devices have limited communication and processing capabilities due to the energy consuming communication, small physical factors, battery operations, and long lifetime expectations. The concept is that, devices transfer data using sensors for communication between them. There are various types of sensors for various purposes. It is difficult to use same protocols for all of them. A multi-protocol receiver is proposed [10]. This receiver retrieves data simultaneously from different communication technologies like WiFi, ZigBee, and Bluetooth. The data is stored and processed in local database (i.e MySQL). For back end analysis, they have used cloud and for transferring data to cloud HTTP has been used. However, the receiver has been used in terms of multi-protocol context. The data was also stored in local machines.

Cloud Computing and IoT are currently two of the most popular ICT paradigms that are expected to shape the next era of computing. The convergence between cloud computing and IoT has become a hot topic over the last few years because of the benefits that IoT could have from the distributed nature of cloud computing infrastructures. This paper [13] proposes a new platform for using cloud computing capacities for provision and support of ubiquitous connectivity and real-time applications and services for smart cities' needs. We present a framework for data procured from highly distributed, heterogeneous, decentralized, real and virtual devices (sensors, actuators, smart devices) that can be automatically managed, analyzed and controlled by distributed cloud-based services.

The authors had proposed IoT and cloud based healthcare system [11]. This was a wearable system. In this system, they had used textile accelerometers, a temperature sensor, a heartbeat chest and Arduino open hardware microcontroller platform called LilyPad. Arduino microcontroller collects data from sensors and data is passed to android-based mobile phone through Bluetooth interface. An application is also developed for android that collects data and sends it to cloud.

HTTP is specifically designed for internet devices not for the constraint devices. In this paper we migrate the local storage to the cloud storage. The intention is alarming one device based on other device. There is no need of intention manager. In order to establish the connection between the sensors and the cloud storage CoAP is used. As devices used (e.g. sensors) are constrained, CoAP is more suited protocol over HTTP. Here multi-protocol receiver system is not required as we will use single device with a single protocol. Researchers used local database for storing data. Here storage is cloud.

In this paper sensors will be connected through WiFi. The data will be stored and processed in cloud. As the sensor will act on processed data that are being sent from cloud intention manager is not required. Additional hardware requirements are eliminated (e.g. local storage devices). This reduces the cost and helps to prevent hardware revisions. As the data is automatically passing from one sensor to another, there is no need of user interaction. Here CoAP is used as an application layer protocol. CoAP is more suited to very small sensor deployments with tiny hardware and completely different security.

3 System Architecture

The proposed architecture is depicted in Fig. 1. The step by step functionality of the proposed architecture is explained as follows:

i We have used two sensors as shown in the architecture given in the Fig. 1 for fire detection and for controlling the door (i.e. Alerting the door to be opened if fire exists).
ii In order to connect the sensors to the Internet for exchanging the data Arduino is used as an intermediate device. Arduino will be programmed to

perform the required task. Arduino and the sensors are connected through a WiFi shield.

iii CoAP protocol is used for exchanging data between sensors through cloud.
iv The fire/smoke detector will store the sensed data into the cloud storage, where the status of the sensor is stored to point out the existence of fire.
v The sensor attached with the door is responsible to alert the door to be opened in case the existence of fire. This sensor will be getting the alert information regarding fire existence from the cloud storage. The door sensor will be continuously checking the status of the fire sensor, if it detects the status to be on (i.e Indication of existence of fire) immediately smart doors will be opened for the exit.
vi For Cloud Service there can be several platforms (e.g. Google Cloud, Thingspeak, 000Webhost, Amazon, Microsoft Azure etc.). In our work, we will use Google cloud for getting the cloud facilities.

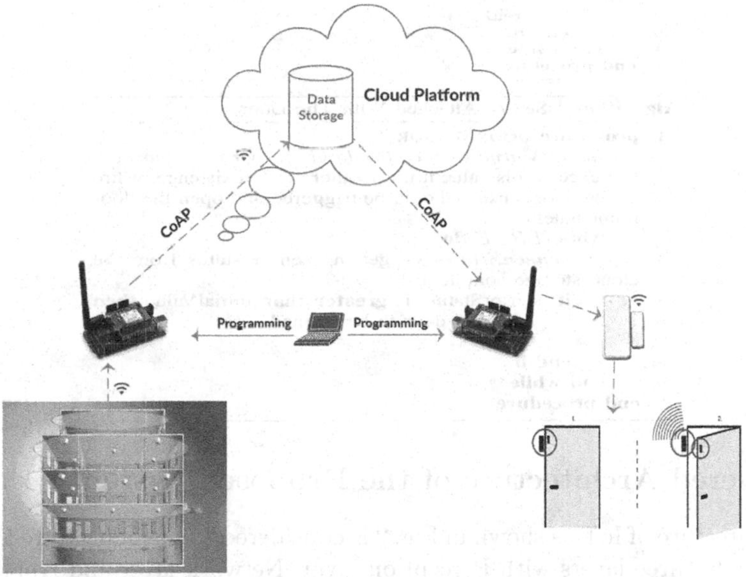

Fig. 1. Proposed architecture of harmonizing IoT in Cloud.

4 Algorithmic Analysis

We have proposed two algorithms to show the overall functionality of the system.

Algorithm 1 for smoke detector shows the overall responsibility and the functionality of the smoke sensor. The variable sensor status given in Algorithm 1, shows the status of the smoke sensor. This variable is shared between the smoke sensor and the sensor attached with the door. As given in the algorithm, the sensor is sensing the environment continuously and if the sensor's sensed value is greater than defined threshold value (i.e. Indication of fire existence) then it will update its status (i.e. Shared variable) in the storage.

The Algorithm 2 explains that how the sensor attached with door will get notification regarding existence of fire. The sensor attached with the door is continuously checking the status (i.e. shared variable) of the smoke sensor and if it finds out that the value of the shared variable is greater than defined threshold value then immediately it will alert the door to be opened for the fire exit.

Algorithm 1 Smoke Detector

```
procedure SMOKESENSOR
    unLock the sensorStatus variable in the cloud
    initialValue ← the standard temperature value assigned to sensor    ▷ if it exceed this value it means there is an existence of fire so the door sensors should be triggered.
    while TRUE do
        sensedData ← sensing the environment
        if sensedData is greater than initialValue then
            sensorStatus ← sensedData    ▷ update the sensor status in the cloud
            Lock the sensorStatus variable in the cloud so that no sensor could update it within this period of fire exit
            break
        end if
    end while
end procedure
```

Algorithm 2 Sensor Attached With The Door

```
procedure DOORSENSOR
    initialValue ← the standard temperature value    ▷ if it exceed this value it means there is an existence of fire so the door sensors should be triggered and open the door immediately.
    while TRUE do
        sensedStatus ← get the sensor status from the cloud storage continuously
        if sensorStatus is greater than initialValue then
            Alert the door to be opened
            break
        end if
    end while
end procedure
```

5 Layered Architecture of the Proposed System

The architecture of IoT as shown in Fig. 2 is considered to be multilayered. There are basically three layers with Perception layer, Network layer and Application layer. There are two more layers: Middleware layer and Business layer [7,8].

Perception Layer. Perception layer is the lowest layer of the architecture. The main task of this layer is to sense the data. At first the object must be identified and then collect the data from the objects for example sensors. In our model, fire sensor will continuously sense the environment to figure out the existence of fire.

Network Layer. From Perception layer data is passed to network layer. Network layer gathers data from lower layer and sends it to the Internet. In network layer there is a gateway, with two interfaces, one connected to the sensor and other to the Internet [6].

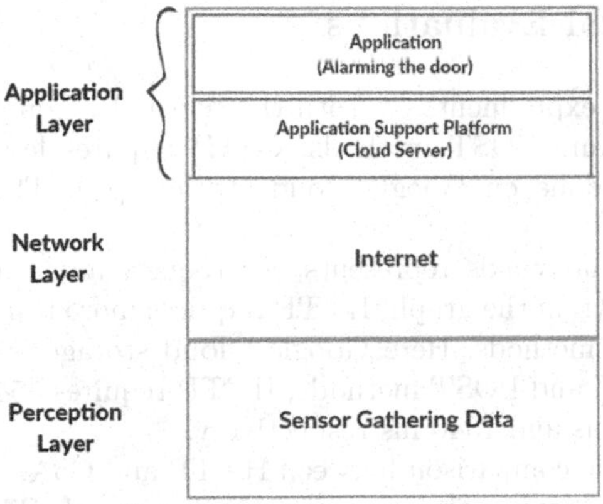

Fig. 2. Layered architecture of harmonizing IoT.

Application Layer. Application layer is for the user level interaction, it provides the service for the collected data from the sensors. This layer consists of application support platform and concrete applications [7]. In our proposed model the application layer has been divided into two parts, the application itself and application layer support platform.

Application (Alarming the door). This part will provide the service of opening the door in case of any emergency exit due to existence of fire in the building.

Application Support Platform. We have used Cloud Server as an application support platform for the end sensors.

6 Way of Implementation

Data from IoT pass to cloud for being stored and later on the stored data is used in order to perform the desired task (i.e. alerting the door to be opened in case of any fire existence). Source Code for the implementation is written in arduino programming and is installed into a WiFi arduino shield to interact with the devices. Devices for example sensors produce a lot of data at every moment. It is irrelevant to store all the data as it is not necessary. In order to overcome this problem a smart gateway would help for better utilization of data and cloud resources [4]. There are two types of architecture for web services, REpresentational State Transfer (REST) and Service-Oriented Architecture (SOA). SOAs are often used to model and realize complex business flows. In this paper REST architecture is used. The RESTful protocols are CoAP and HTTP. HTTP uses HTTP-similar standardized methods. For interacting with things for example doors and sensors, CoAP is used which is designed for constrained devices. Many commercial and open source platforms are available for IoT and cloud implementation [5].

7 Experimental Evaluations

We have done some experiments on both the methods. Comparing CoAP with HTTP using GET and POST methods, CoAP requires less amount of time. The experiment is done on Google cloud storage [15], Thingspeak [16] and 000webhost [17].

Figure 3 x-axis and y-axis represents per request and time in milliseconds respectively. As shown in the graph, HTTP requires more time than CoAP both in GET and POST methods. Here Google Cloud storage is used to store the data. In case of GET and POST methods, HTTP requires 554 ms, 1520 ms and CoAP requires 367 ms and 1346 ms respectively.

Figure 4 shows the comparison between HTTP and CoAP when Thingspeak storage is used. As shown in the graph for GET method, HTTP requires 1902 ms where CoAP requires 1696 ms and in case of POST method, HTTP requires 1266 ms where CoAP requires 1013 ms.

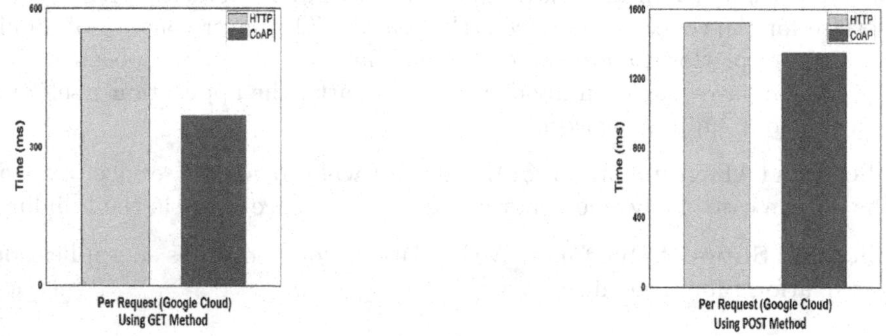

Fig. 3. Comparison of HTTP and CoAP protocols based on GET and POST method using Google Cloud as a Storage.

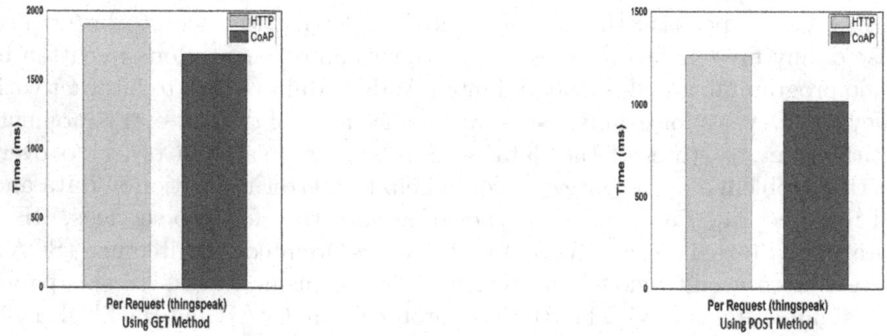

Fig. 4. Comparison of HTTP and CoAP protocols based on GET and POST method using Thingspeak as a Storage.

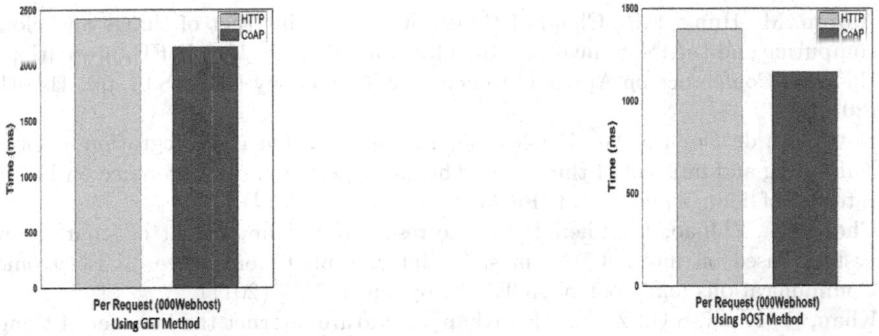

Fig. 5. Comparison of HTTP and CoAP protocols based on GET and POST method using 000webhost as a Storage.

Figure 5 shows that for GET and POST methods, HTTP requires 2415 ms, 1389 ms and CoAP requires 2161 ms, 1154 ms respectively using 000webhost as a storage.

Finally we can say that in each stage of comparison HTTP is more time consuming while interacting through GET and POST methods. We have introduced the implementation of our work using CoAP where it requires less time and is faster than HTTP.

8 Conclusions and Future Works

In this paper we present an idea to harmonize two sensors such that they will interact with each other and act on output produced by one of the sensor. One is to detect the existence of fire and the other one acts on the output of the fire detector sensor. Which is used to control the door in case of existence of fire. Here we have stored the sensed data in the cloud. We do not have local storage. Hence the system becomes cloud based. In our implementation the performance has been increased compared to the existing system. In our future work, we are going to implement and commission the proposed idea in a smart environment for commercial uses.

References

1. Islam, M.M., Huh, E.-N.: Sensor proxy mobile IPv6 (SPMIPv6) – a novel scheme for mobility supported IP-WSNs. Sensors **2**(11), 1865–1887 (2011)
2. Islam, M.M., Huh, E.-N.: A novel addressing scheme for PMIPv6 based global IP-WSNs. Sensors **11**(9), 8430–8455 (2011)
3. Kum, S.W., Moon, J., Lim, T., Park, J.: A novel design of IoT cloud delegate framework to harmonize cloud-scale IoT services. IEEE International Conference on Consumer Electronics (ICCE), pp. 247–248 (2015)

4. Aazam, M., Hung, P.P.: Cloud of things integrating internet of things and cloud computing and the issues involved. In: The proceedings of 11th IEEE International Bhurban Conference on Applied Sciences and Technology (IBCAST), pp. 414–419 (2014)
5. Botta, A., de Donato, W., Persico, V., Pescapé, A.: On the integration of cloud computing and internet of things. In: The 2nd International Conference on Future Internet of Things and Cloud (FiCloud), pp. 23–30 (2014)
6. Chong, G., Zhihao, L., Yifeng, Y.: The research and implement of smart home system based on internet of things. In: International Conference on Electronics Communications and Control (ICECC), pp. 2944–2947 (2011)
7. Khan, R., Khan, S.U., Zaheer, R., Khan, S.: Future internet the internet of things architecture, possible applications and key challenges. In: 10th International Conference on Frontiers of Information Technology (FIT), pp. 257–260 (2012)
8. Wu, M., Lu, T.-J., Ling, F.-Y., Sun, J., Du, H.-Y.: Research on the architecture of Internet of things. In: 3rd International Conference on Advanced Computer Theory and Engineering (ICACTE), vol. 5, pp. V5–484 (2010)
9. Gunasagarana, R., et al.: Internet of things sensor to sensor communication. In: IEEE Sensors, pp. 1–4 (2015)
10. Su, J.-H., Lee, C.-S., Wu, W.-C.: The design and implementation of a low-cost and programmable home automation module. IEEE Trans. Consum. Electron. **52**(4), 1239–1244 (2006)
11. Levä, T., Mazhelis, O., Suomi, H.: Comparing the cost-efficiency of CoAP and HTTP in Web of Things applications. Decis. Support Syst. **63**, 23–38 (2014)
12. Daniel, L., Kojo, M., Latvala, M.: Experimental evaluation of the CoAP, HTTP and SPDY transport services for internet of things. In: Fortino, G., Di Fatta, G., Li, W., Ochoa, S., Cuzzocrea, A., Pathan, M. (eds.) IDCS 2014. LNCS, vol. 8729, pp. 111–123. Springer, Cham (2014). https://doi.org/10.1007/978-3-319-11692-1_10
13. Suciu, G., Vulpe, A., Halunga, S., Fratu, O., Todoran, G., Suciu, V.: Smart cities built on resilient cloud computing and secure internet of things. In: 19th International Conference Control Systems and Computer Science (CSCS), pp. 513–518 (2013)
14. Zanella, A., Bui, N., Castellani, A., Vangelista, L., Zorzi, M.: Internet of things for smart cities. IEEE Internet Things J. **1**(1), 22–32 (2014)
15. Google Cloud Homepage. https://www.cloud.google.com. Accessed 20 Feb 2018
16. Thingspeak Homepage. https://www.thingspeak.com. Accessed 20 Feb 2018
17. 000Webhost Homepage. https://www.000webhost.com. Accessed 20 Feb 2018
18. Thangavel, D., Ma, X., Valera, A., Tan, H.X., Tan, C.K.: Performance evaluation of MQTT and CoAP via a common middleware. In: IEEE Ninth International Conference on Intelligent Sensors Sensor Networks and Information Processing (ISSNIP), pp. 1–6 (2014)

IoT Big Data Analytics with Fog Computing for Household Energy Management in Smart Grids

Shailendra Singh[1] and Abdulsalam Yassine[2(✉)]

[1] Department of Electrical and Computer Engineering, Lakehead University, 955 Oliver Road, Thunder Bay, ON P7B 5E1, Canada
ssingh59@lakeheadu.ca

[2] Department of Software Engineering, Lakehead University, 955 Oliver Road, Thunder Bay, ON P7B 5E1, Canada
ayassine@lakeheadu.ca

Abstract. Smart homes generate a vast amount of data measurements from smart meters and devices. These data have all the velocity and veracity characteristics to be called as Big Data. Meter data analytics holds tremendous potential for utilities to understand customers' energy consumption patterns, and allows them to manage, plan, and optimize the operation of the power grid efficiently. In this paper, we propose a unified architecture that enables innovative operations for near real-time processing of large fine-grained energy consumption data. Specifically, we propose an Internet of Things (IoT) big data analytics system that makes use of fog computing to address the challenges of complexities and resource demands for near real-time data processing, storage, and classification analysis. The design architecture and requirements of the proposed framework are illustrated in this paper while the analytics components are validated using datasets acquired from real homes.

Keywords: Internet of Things · Cloud computing · Fog computing
Big data analytics · Energy management · Smart grids

1 Introduction

The combination of IoT and big data analytics technology is expected to shape the decision-making processes in various industries [1]. As IoT systems expand to smart city applications that demand instantaneous actions, processing enormous data in near real-time to satisfy the stringent requirements of smart city functions becomes a challenging prospect. One solution is to use cloud-based systems since there is an abundance of computing and storage resources for various computationally intensive applications that need processing of high volume of data on the fly. However, attaining real-time responses from a cloud system is practically difficult due to the inherited latency of the underlying transport

A.-S. K. Pathan et al. (Eds.): SGIoT 2018, LNICST 256, pp. 13–22, 2019.
https://doi.org/10.1007/978-3-030-05928-6_2

communication network which has significant impact on time-sensitive applications [2–5]. Fog computing fundamentally resolves latency issues by processing and storing data at the edge of the cloud system [3,6]. Furthermore, fog computing nodes are resource-efficient because they are equipped with virtual machine technologies capable of continuously processing fresh IoT streams of data and transfer the processed data to the cloud for further processing. These nodes play a key role in the IoT ecosystem to support the processing of big data for near real-time responses. As a result, IoT big data analytics begin to leverage fog computing infrastructure to handle the data on the fly, with low latency.

In this paper, we propose a unified architecture that enables innovative operations for near real-time processing of enormous fine-grained data. As a compelling application of such architecture, we focus on developing a scalable IoT big data analytics with fog computing for processing and analyzing household energy consumption data for smart grids. Through smart meters and sensor devices, households generate continuous streams of massive amount of data in short time intervals. A large part of these data is attributed to home appliances and plug-in electric vehicles. Processing and analyzing these data is vital for smart grid energy management applications that aim at reducing cost and greenhouse gas emissions [7,8]. However, the implementation of home data analytics can be quite costly for a large number of consumers. The total computational effort required to perform data analytics for each consumer over time at fine-grained intervals is enormous. This is extremely challenging for utilities trying to adopt analytics to find the right consumers for an energy management program, let alone the heterogeneity of consumers' energy consumption behaviors [12,13]. To cope with such analytics complexities, several research studies, such as those in [10,11,15,18] and [19], have proposed IoT platforms with dedicated resources from fog and edge computing nodes to perform the analytical computations. The main idea is to be as close as possible to the source where data is generated. While such approaches are genuine, they tackle the latency issue only, but not necessarily applicable for handling a large volume of incoming data that requires orchestration of various application requirements. For example, residential Automatic Demand Response (ADR) applications require energy consumption data about appliances in residential homes to be analyzed in near real-time to engage them in demand response signals effectively [9]. Other smart grid applications that require predictive analytics need access to historical data which must be stored in a large database that only can be provided by a cloud system [14].

We present an Internet of Things (IoT) big data analytics platform with fog computing that is capable of managing, analyzing and transforming household energy consumption data into actionable insights. The proposed system, which acts as a hub for metered consumption and event data originating from household energy systems, is well suited to support huge data and computationally-intensive, always-on applications. It addresses the challenges of complexities and resource demands for near real-time data processing as well as the requirements of scalability with the growing volume of data and the temporal granularity of decision making. The advantages of such a platform lie in the ability of serving multiple households within a neighborhood at the same time which means that we can process multiple home appliances in parallel. Thus allowing us to analyze data faster and engage home appliances in smart grid applications (e.g. ADR) in a timely manner.

The rest of the paper is organized as follows: In Sect. 2, we present the components of the proposed platform followed by a study case in Sect. 3. Finally, in Sect. 4 we conclude the paper and provide direction for future work.

2 Platform Overview

2.1 Requirements and Functionalities

As mentioned earlier, utility companies are facing simultaneous streams of data from multiple household devices and metering systems. The design of an innovative platform that is suited to support a huge amount of energy for smart grid energy management applications posses peculiar requirements, functionalities, and design structures.

- IoT energy metering streams should be handled in a parallel manner to boost the performance of data analytics and to optimize the smart grid dynamic energy management operations. Depending on the analytics activity, the specific requirements include elastic resource acquisition, efficient data network management, data reliability, and functional data abstractions.
- Data processing should make full use of all computational resources to address performance challenges of near real-time computation algorithms such as finding hidden patterns and produce new, faster and richer knowledge.
- Home appliance data changes over time due to the changing consumption behavior of consumers. As a result, an automated data ingestion pipeline must support dynamic data acquisition at variable rates and volumes and be adaptive to current data sources and operational needs. This high-speed pipeline should process all incoming time-series data, applies simple data transformations, and outputs the processed data.

The main challenges for satisfying the above requirements especially for near real-time energy management applications are in the development of a platform capable of processing and analyzing large volume of energy consumption data streaming from various sources. Next section describes the proposed platform.

2.2 Platform Components

In Fig. 1, we present an IoT big data analytics with fog computing platform that supports complex operation of continuous integration, processing and analytics of multiple household energy consumption data.

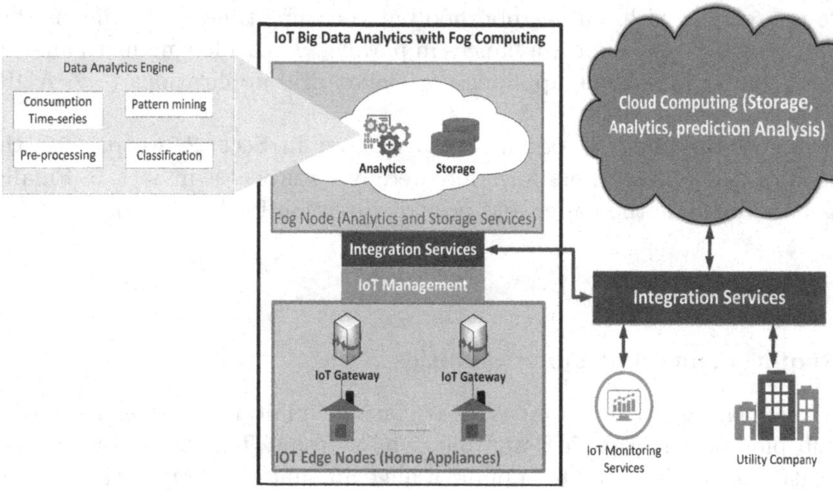

Fig. 1. IoT big data analytics with fog computing

The architecture is mainly composed of four sub-systems that enable the management of household energy consumption data in near real-time. These modules are as follows:

- **IoT data acquisition**: In the proposed model, data is acquired from household appliances through data acquisition modules or the smart meter disaggregated data services. In either case, IoT protocols such as machine-to-machine (M2M)/Internet of Things (MQTT) are responsible for transporting the data between home appliances and the IoT gateway. An IoT gateway acts as a broker that connects IoT home devices to the IoT management entity that bridges the communication to the fog nodes.
- **IoT Management and Integration Services**: The IoT management services play a mediating role for transferring data from IoT devices to Fog computing nodes and then to the cloud system. They are protocol independent and are mainly responsible for maintaining continuity and flexibility for the whole IoT ecosystem. The frequency of data transfer is generally application specific. For example, smart meter data are collected in intervals of 15 min with various resolutions. The integration services provide application programming interfaces (APIs) with external systems. There are many benefits for decoupling the analytical components of the fog nodes from the external systems. Such decoupling assures security since users would not be able to have any direct access to the analytical engine. Also, it adds abstracting data and interoperability by enabling the use of data for various user-specific applications including mobile and desktop applications.
- **Fog Computing Nodes**: The fog node is a resource-efficient computational entity that supports rapid analytics of energy consumption data for near real-time smart grid applications. Among the main function of the fog node

is pre-processing collected IoT data and sending the aggregated results to the cloud or directly to the serviced applications. By doing so, the fog nodes increase the ability of the platform to manage an integrated array of analytics for smart grid applications in highly automated ways which result in significant savings for the grid operator. Also, utilities can design and develop their applications using fog nodes that offer abundance elasticity to enhance performance, redundancy and storage devices that make the scaling problem of energy consumption analytics much easier to handle. We should note that the method of allocating fog nodes to households is beyond the scope of this paper. However, optimization mechanisms such as those in [16,17] may be employed to determine the optimal distribution and configuration of fog nodes while taking into consideration the computational resources and capability of processing the required data from multiple homes. In the case of configuring more than one household to a single fog node, privacy and security of information is often considered an issue which can be tackled by mechanisms such as those in [20,21,23,24] and [25] should be considered.

- **Cloud System**: Household energy consumption management and data analytics is a complex operation that requires continuous integration of multiple sources to a common processing system with easy access to data. In the proposed platform, energy consumption from many fog nodes is aggregated at the cloud system which provides additional computations for large data processing.

2.3 Data Analytics Engine

The data analytics engine in our platform performs all the short-term analytics at the edge of the cloud system. Energy consumption time-series data acquired from IoT streams are processed as they arrive at the analytical engine. The processing of this data can be divided into three main stages: pre-processing, pattern mining, and classification.

In pre-processing stage all IoT streams are filtered, parsed and translated into a unified data structure for further analysis. At this stage, raw data which contains millions of high time-resolution energy records are transformed into a pre-defined resolution for each appliance, while recording usage duration, average load, and energy consumption. The decision for determining the resolution (5 min, 15 min, 30 min, etc.) is provided and configured by the user. In the second stage, frequent pattern mining techniques are conducted on the data to discover the occurrence of appliance correlation in a dataset. The main idea here is to uncover appliance relationships that affect energy consumption behavior. Frequent pattern mining searches for these recurring patterns in a given dataset to determine associations and correlations among patterns of interest [22]. In our platform, the data analytics engine uses both the FP-growth mechanism and the Apriori algorithm to discover appliance associations in the form of frequent patterns and association rules, respectively.

In clustering stage, we employ an unsupervised form of classification which is capable of distinguishing classes of appliances which are learned from the data [22]. There are various clustering approaches such as hierarchical clustering, centroid-based or partitional distribution clustering, distribution-based clustering, and density-based clustering. In our model, we extend the k-means, which is a partitional distribution clustering algorithm, to discover appliance-time associations. Our goal is to provide a critical analysis of consumer energy consumption behavior concerning preferences on time of energy usage. Appliance-time associations can be defined with respect to hour of day, time of day, weekday, week, month and/or season. Determining the appliance-time associations, for an appliance, can be considered as a grouping of sufficiently close appliance usage time-stamps, when that appliance has been recorded as active or operational, to form classes or clusters. The clusters or classes constructed will describe appliance-time associations while respective size of clusters, defined as the count of members in the cluster, will establish the relative strength for the clusters. The strength or size of the cluster will indicate how frequently and when a given appliance has been used by consumer, which indicate personal preferences. Therefore, discovery of appliance-time associations can be translated into clustering of appliances' operating time-stamps into brackets of time-spans, where each cluster belongs to an appliance with respective time-stamps (data points) as members of the cluster. Finally, the results of the above mentioned stages are send to the cloud system which is freed for computationally intensive tasks, especially where the analysis of historical data and large datasets is concerned.

3 Case Study and Analysis

We conducted extensive experiments using household energy consumption data from smart meters using the real dataset [26]. We present sample results indicative of our observations. Figures 2 and 3 show the energy consumption patterns for Toaster and Home Theater over hour-of-day, time-of-day, weekday, month and season. The outcome of the frequent pattern mining is the association among appliances that are the result of the simultaneous use of the appliance by occupants. Figure 4 show the result of clustering operation that is part of possible behavioral predictive analytics, which can be conducted at fog nodes. The figure exhibit, appliance to hour-of-day associations for Toaster that were determined by clustering of the time-stamps where the toaster was registered operating. Further, when we compare Figs. 2 and 4, we notice that the outcome of clustering analysis successfully captures the appliance usage patterns that are direct reflection of occupants energy consumption behavior. This is in addition to the appliance-to-appliance associations learned through frequent pattern mining that comprehensively represent energy usage behavioral traits of occupants. Similar results were obtained for appliance to time-of-day, weekday, month and season associations. Further, it can be done while taking into account the local energy generation through renewal sources at individual house or a neighborhood level. By facilitating distributed near real-time smart meter big data analytics at

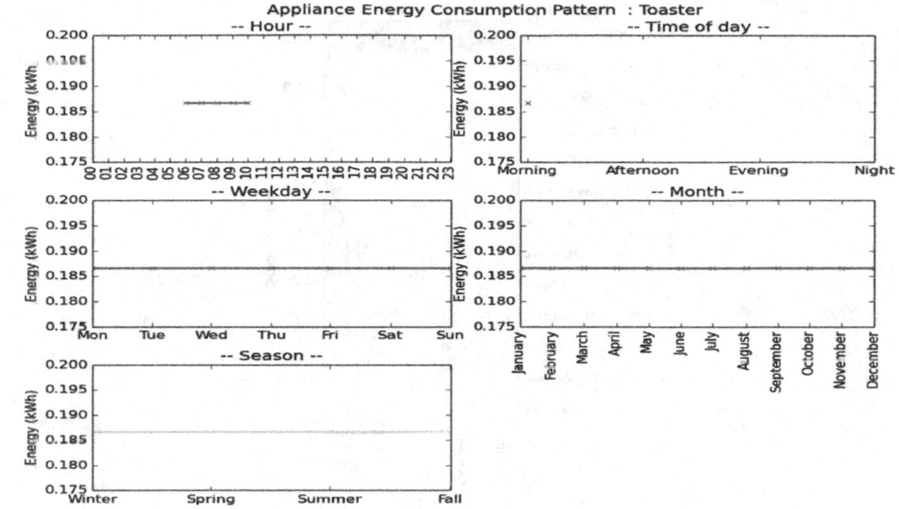

Fig. 2. Energy consumption pattern - Toaster

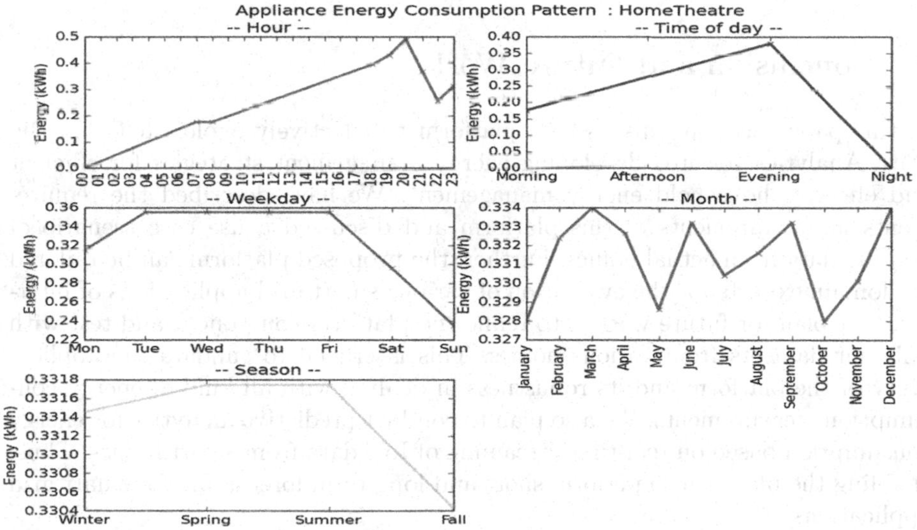

Fig. 3. Energy consumption pattern - Home theater

the edge of the cloud using fog computing the proposed platform can aid effective and in-time decision making for individual house owners, distribution whereas large-scale data analytics in the cloud can facilitate various energy management programs at producers level.

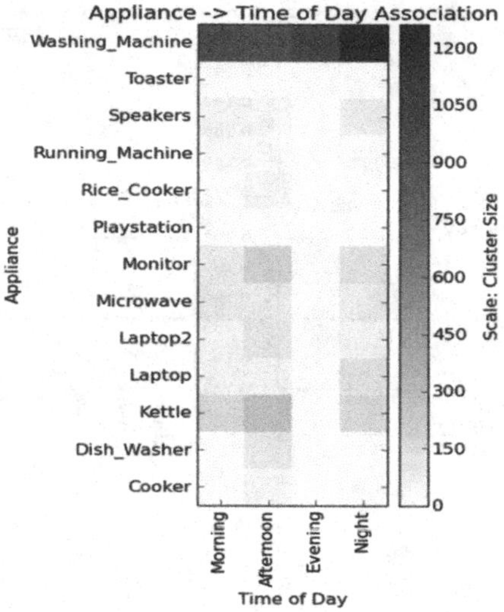

Fig. 4. Appliance time of the day associations. It shows the co-utilization of appliances during the day

4 Conclusion and Future Work

In this paper, we have discussed a platform to effectively exploit IoT and Big Data Analytics towards developing energy management strategies for efficient and effective household energy management. We have described the requirements and components of this platform and discussed a use case scenario of real-life data from actual homes. Further, the proposed platform can be tailored by domain experts for the evaluation of various smart grid applications of interest. Our plan for future work is to refine the platform component and test with different datasets from various homes. This is crucial to validate the applicability of the platform and its robustness in dealing with all kind of energy consumption measurements. We also plan to conduct predictive analytics for energy consumption based on real-time streaming of IoT data from smart homes. Thus, enabling the platform to perform short and long term forecasting for smart grid applications.

References

1. Chhabra, A.S., Choudhury, T., Srivastava, A.V., Aggarwal, A.: Prediction for big data and IoT in 2017. In: International Conference on Infocom Technologies and Unmanned Systems (Trends and Future Directions) (ICTUS), Dubai, pp. 181-187 (2017)
2. Ge, Y., Liang, X., Zhou, Y.C., Pan, Z., Zhao, G.T., Zheng, Y.L.: Adaptive analytic service for real-time internet of things applications. In: IEEE International Conference on Web Services (ICWS), San Francisco, CA, pp. 484–491 (2016)

3. El-Sayed, H., et al.: Edge of Things: The big picture on the integration of edge, IoT and the cloud in a distributed computing environment. IEEE Access **6**, 1706–1717 (2018)
4. Pouladzadeh, P., Kuhad, P., Peddi, S.V.B., Yassine, A., Shirmohammadi, S.: Mobile cloud based food calorie measurement. In: IEEE International Conference on Multimedia and Expo Workshops (ICMEW), Chengdu, pp. 1–6 (2014)
5. Peddi, S.V.B., Kuhad, P., Yassine, A., Pouladzadeh, P., Shirmohammadi, S., Shirehjini, A.A.N.: An intelligent cloud-based data processing broker for mobile e-health multimedia applications. Future Generat. Comput. Syst. J. **66**, 71–86 (2017)
6. Mebrek, A., Merghem-Boulahia, L., Esseghir, M.: Efficient green solution for a balanced energy consumption and delay in the IoT-Fog-Cloud computing. In: IEEE 16th International Symposium on Network Computing and Applications (NCA), Cambridge, pp. 1-4 (2017)
7. Al-Ali, A.R., Zualkernan, I.A., Rashid, M., Gupta, R., Alikarar, M.: A smart home energy management system using IoT and big data analytics approach. IEEE Trans. Consum. Electron. **63**(4), 426–434 (2017)
8. Berouine, A., Lachhab, F., Malek, Y.N., Bakhouya, M., Ouladsine, R.: A smart metering platform using big data and IoT technologies. In: 3rd International Conference of Cloud Computing Technologies and Applications (CloudTech), Rabat, pp. 1-6 (2017)
9. Yassine, A.: Implementation challenges of automatic demand response for households in smart grids. In: 3rd International Conference on Renewable Energies for Developing Countries (REDEC), Zouk Mosbeh, pp. 1–6 (2016)
10. Sultan, M., Ahmed, K.N.: SLASH: self-learning and adaptive smart home framework by integrating IoT with big data analytics. In: Computing Conference, London, pp. 530–538 (2017)
11. Yang, S.: IoT stream processing and analytics in the fog. IEEE Commun. Mag. **55**(8), 21–27 (2017)
12. Singh, S., Yassine, A.: Big data mining of energy time series for behavioral analytics and energy consumption forecasting. Energies **11**, 452 (2018)
13. Singh, S., Yassine, A.: Mining energy consumption behavior patterns for households in smart grid. IEEE Transactions on Emerging Topics in Computing (2017). https://doi.org/10.1109/TETC.2017.2692098
14. Cai, H., Xu, B., Jiang, L., Vasilakos, A.V.: IoT-based big data storage systems in cloud computing: perspectives and challenges. IEEE Internet Things J. **4**(1), 75–87 (2017)
15. He, J., Wei, J., Chen, K., Tang, Z., Zhou, Y., Zhang, Y.: Multi-tier fog computing with large-scale IoT data analytics for smart cities. IEEE Internet Things J. **5**(2), 677–686 (2018). https://doi.org/10.1109/JIOT.2017.2724845
16. Taneja, M., Davy, A.: Resource aware placement of IoT application modules in Fog-Cloud Computing Paradigm. In: IFIP/IEEE Symposium on Integrated Network and Service Management (IM), Lisbon, pp. 1222-1228 (2017)
17. Minh, Q.T., Nguyen, D.T., Van Le, A., Nguyen, H.D., Truong, A.: Toward service placement on Fog computing landscape. In: 4th NAFOSTED Conference on Information and Computer Science, Hanoi, pp. 291–296 (2017)
18. Gonzalez, N.M., et al.: Fog computing: data analytics and cloud distributed processing on the network edges. In: 35th International Conference of the Chilean Computer Science Society (SCCC), Valparaiíso, pp. 1-9 (2016)

19. Cao, H., Wachowicz, M., Cha, S.: Developing an edge computing platform for real-time descriptive analytics. In: IEEE International Conference on Big Data (Big Data), Boston, MA, pp. 4546–4554 (2017)
20. Yassine, A., Nazari Shirehjini, A.A., Shirmohammadi, S.: Smart meters big data: game theoretic model for fair data sharing in deregulated smart grids. IEEE Access **vol. 3, no**, 2743–2754 (2015)
21. Yassine, A., Shirmohammadi, S.: Measuring user's privacy payoff using intelligent agents. In: IEEE International Conference on Computational Intelligence for Measurement Systems and Applications, CIMSA 2009, pp 169–174 (2009)
22. Han, J., Pei, J., kamber, M.: Mining Frequent Patterns, Associations, and Correlations: Basic Concepts and Methods. Data mining: Concepts and techniques, Chap. 6, 3rd edn, pp. 243–278. Morgan Kaufmann, Waltham (2011). http://www.sciencedirect.com/science/book/9780123814791. ISBN: 9780123814791
23. Paverd, A., Martin, A., Brown, I.: Security and privacy in smart grid demand response systems. In: Cuellar, J. (ed.) SmartGridSec 2014. LNCS, vol. 8448, pp. 1–15. Springer, Cham (2014). https://doi.org/10.1007/978-3-319-10329-7_1
24. Yassine, A., Shirmohammadi, S.: Privacy and the market for private data: a negotiation model to capitalize on private data. In: IEEE/ACS International Conference on Computer Systems and Applications, Doha, pp. 669-678 (2008)
25. Yassine, A., Shirehjini, A.A., Shirmohammadi, S., Tran, T.: Knowledge-empowered agent information system for privacy payoff in ecommerce. Knowl. Inf. Syst. **32**(2), 445–473 (2012)
26. Makonin, S., Ellert, B., Bajic, I.V., Popowich, F.: AMPds2 - Almanac of minutely power dataset : electricity, water, and natural gas consumption of a residential house in Canada from 2012 to 2014. Sci. Data **3**, 1–12 (2015). https://doi.org/10.1038/sdata.2016.37

Secured Cancer Care and Cloud Services in IoT/WSN Based Medical Systems

Adeniyi Onasanya(✉) and Maher Elshakankiri

Department of Computer Science, University of Regina, Regina, SK S4S 0A2, Canada
{Onasanya,Maher.Elshakankiri}@uregina.ca

Abstract. In recent years, the Internet of Things (IoT) has constituted a driving force of modern technological advancement, and it has become increasingly common as its impacts are seen in a variety of application domains, including healthcare. IoT is characterized by the interconnectivity of smart sensors, objects, devices, data, and applications. With the unprecedented use of IoT in industrial, commercial and domestic, it becomes very imperative to harness the benefits and functionalities associated with the IoT technology in (re)assessing the provision and positioning of healthcare to ensure efficient and improved healthcare delivery. In this research, we are focusing on two important services in healthcare systems, which are cancer care services and business analytics/cloud services. These services incorporate the implementation of an IoT that provides solution and framework for analyzing health data gathered from IoT through various sensor networks and other smart devices in order to improve healthcare delivery and to help health care providers in their decision-making process for enhanced and efficient cancer treatment. In addition, we discuss the wireless sensor network (WSN), WSN routing and data transmission in the healthcare environment. Finally, some operational challenges and security issues with IoT-based healthcare system are discussed.

Keywords: IoT · Smart health care system
(wireless) Sensor network · Cancer care services · Cloud services
Business analytics

1 Introduction

Internet of Things (IoT) technology presents promising technological, economic, and social benefits to the evolution of data communications and networking facilities due to the advanced connectivity of devices, systems, and services beyond machine-to-machine (M2M) communications. Interestingly, the IoT technology has contributed to and supported a wide range of services and applications, such as smart cities, waste management, home automation, transportation systems, and healthcare. It is also fuelling the development of "smart connected things" – televisions, thermostats, medical devices, cars, wearable technology – clothing and devices [7].

A.-S. K. Pathan et al. (Eds.): SGIoT 2018, LNICST 256, pp. 23–35, 2019.
https://doi.org/10.1007/978-3-030-05928-6_3

This research considers two of the various services that are pertinent to healthcare delivery. Specifically, it is intended to propose the application and implementation of IoT technology in cancer care health delivery in the context of cancer care services along with the incorporation of business analytics and cloud services for cancer care treatments and diagnoses. The combination of these services proffers solution and framework for analyzing health data gathered from IoT through various sensor networks and other smart connected devices to help healthcare providers to turn a stream of data into actionable insights and evidence-based healthcare decision making about the health conditions of patients using appropriate analytics tools to improve and enhance cancer treatments.

1.1 Motivation and Related Work

The motivation for this research work has been triggered by the desire to improve the cancer care in healthcare delivery. Hence, this has prompted the need to (re)assess the provision and positioning of healthcare services to harness the benefits associated with the use of IoT technology. This relatively new trend in IoT technology will suffice in ensuring interconnectivity and interoperability among the health centres, clinics, and hospitals in various regions through network design that will facilitate health region-wide communications. As a result, it is argued that the use of IoT initiative will offer huge benefits such as increased workforce productivity, overall cost savings, enhanced Return on Investment (ROI), improved and new business models [12], and improved collaboration with health practitioners and patients in every service of healthcare delivery. It is also argued that by 2019, about 87% of healthcare organizations would have adopted IoT technology with about 76% in the healthcare industry [17]. The widespread application of IoT in healthcare domain has been successfully applied in a variety of services, including cancer care and business analytics/cloud services [8], medical system (such as clinical care – drug labelling and administration, blood transfusion, real-time ECG monitoring, etc.) [7,10], health and wellness monitoring, remote monitoring system [11], rehabilitation system [3], operational services system [2,4], emergency services system [4,9], just to mention a few. In the course of this research work, we found that most of the papers only mentioned some of the services listed above but none on the application of IoT in cancer care services until a brief version of our initial work [8] has been published. In essence, we have incorporated lots of details and proposed new frameworks, components, and benefits not previously covered in the implementation of IoT and cloud services in cancer care services in this research.

1.2 Background of Smart Healthcare System

Adoption of IoT based healthcare systems in all the operations of health industry will facilitate enhanced diagnoses/treatments and monitoring, automatic infirmity and condition detecting and sensing, community health care, location-based health care, rehabilitation, surgery and recovery, imaging services, etc. The IoT devices will be used for communicating between patients and those in the circle of care, and for sharing and interconnecting healthcare network resources into the network as related to the delivery of IoT-based smart healthcare system. The healthcare resources include physicians, doctors, oncologists, health providers, nurses, other health personnel in the circle of care, patients, caregivers, human resources, ambulances, emergency units, medical devices, hospital sites, clinics, community health centres, workstation servers, smart devices or connected things (e.g. tablets), sensors, etc. This interconnection of resources can be achieved through various network industry communication standards such as wireless (short, medium and long), Ethernet with transmission control protocol/internet protocol (TCP/IP), unique identifier (UID) based identification, and GPS-based location technologies.

The remainder of the paper is organized as follows. Section 2 discusses the framework for IoT solution. Section 3 provides the methodology and analysis of the network, which includes design basics and hierarchical architecture based on the core, distribution, and access layouts, respectively. Also discussed is the WSN, its routing and data dissemination in the healthcare environment. Section 4 presents the network design solutions for healthcare services using mesh hierarchical topology. Section 5 discusses the concluding remarks and recommendations for future research.

2 IoT Based Healthcare System Framework

Fig. 1 represents an IoT based healthcare system framework for the proposed network that shows the interdependencies of various components that are impacted by the network design methodology. The framework captures some features and approaches to be adopted in presenting the design solution. It also defines the way we integrate, interface, network and transmit the network resources produced by those connected devices from one node to another within the system.

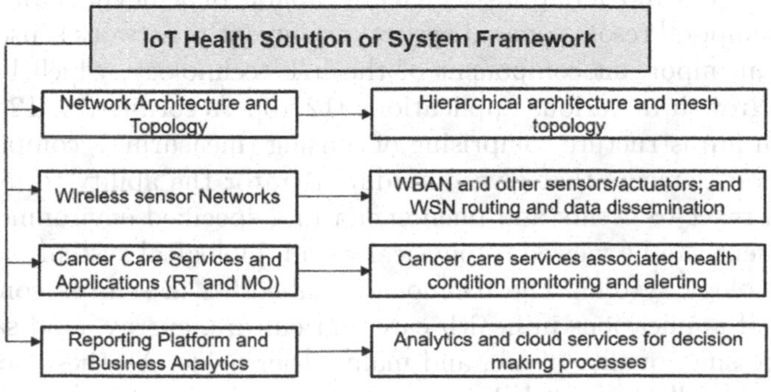

Fig. 1. IoT health solution/system framework.

3 Network Methodology and Analysis

3.1 Network Design Basics and Hierarchical Architecture

It should be noted that the success of any network design is crucial to its implementation. This is why we have paid a close attention to the network design to ensure flaws are eradicated, especially to project of this nature, in terms of the organization size and the number of healthcare network resources that are interconnected. Though, it might be difficult to design a network that is nearly 100% reliable. However, we have thoroughly determined the requirements (i.e. technical and non-technical) in the design of the smart healthcare system in order to decide what is considered a good design, thereby avoiding over complication of the network design.

In addition, two categories of network architecture are considered, namely, *flat architecture* and *hierarchical architecture*, but the focus here is on the hierarchical architecture. Hierarchical architecture is easier to manage and expand, and any inherent issues are more quickly solved with little or no disruption to operation. Typically, hierarchical architecture divides the network into three discrete layers: (1) Core Layout; (2) Distribution Layout; and (3) Access Layout. Each of these layers provides specific functions that define its role within the overall network, thereby resulting in a network that provides modularity with the design goals of scalability (i.e. to meet the demands for additional services), supportability, availability, performance, redundancy, maintainability, security, tolerance, and manageability [5]. The access layer interfaces and controls the end devices (such as sensors, actuators, and IoT connected/smart devices) and the rest of network resources that communicate on the network.

3.2 Wireless Sensor Networks

The combination of the Internet, network communications, information technology, and engineering advances have made provision for a new generation of inexpensive sensors and actuators, which are capable of achieving a high order of spatial and temporal resolution and accuracy. Currently, network sensor systems are seen as an important component of the IoT technology, which has experienced rapid growth in various applications [12,15]. According to [12], a sensor network is an infrastructure comprising of sensing (measuring), computing, and communication elements that gives an administrator the ability to instrument, observe, and react to events and phenomena in a specified environment, where the environment can be viewed as physical world, biological system, or an information technology system. The technology embedded in sensors constitutes a broad range of applications in health care, agriculture, energy, food safety, production processing, quality of life, and many other fields. All these applications involve sensing, collecting, and sharing data.

3.3 WSN Routing and Data Dissemination in Healthcare

Predominantly, the use of wireless/smart sensors and connected devices plays a major part of IoT implementation. These devices are deployed for all the services (with a few exceptions) as they will be strategically attached to or implanted within human body or placed in a specific area to monitor patient under surveillance, treatment or diagnosis in order to collect objective measures/data. Once deployed, the sensor nodes form an autonomous wireless ad hoc network which is attached to the main network.

As the application of WSNs becomes apparently useful for various services in healthcare setting, data and information from sensors are being transmitted and routed within the networks from one site to another, then to the data center site through cloud services (as will be discussed in business analytics and cloud services section). In data dissemination through WSN, some characteristics have to be addressed such as routing protocols from one source to another. This is necessary to adopt appropriate routing strategy in WSNs that is capable of managing the trade-off between optimality and efficiency to ensure computation and communication capabilities [12]. In WSN routing, four strategies are proposed, namely: *flat or hierarchical network*, *structure on the network*, *data-centric network*, and *location network*. But in this research, we consider the location-based routing since it cuts across different locations where the position of the node within the geographical coverage of the network is relevant to query issued by the source node. This ensures cost effective routing approach geographically due to its low overhead and localized interaction [12], and it offers the possibility of including several routing algorithms for data dissemination. The geographical WSN routing and data transmission from WSNs in a clinical setting is illustrated in Fig. 2, where each node of the sensor forwards data to the destination located at the data center within the network.

3.4 Proposed IoT-Based Healthcare Services and Applications

In the design of network, there is a variety of network topologies for network communication. Since the desire is to identify the best solution that meets the needs of a smart healthcare system, a full mesh topology is proposed. In this, every node in the network has a connection to each of the other nodes (i.e. all nodes cooperate in the distribution of data thus allowing for most transmissions to be distributed, even if one of the connections goes down) [5]. The proposed IoT-based healthcare system comprises of services and an array of applications and conditions to patients administered by those in the circle of care. There exists an association between the services and applications/conditions for managing different types of diseases/infirmities, along with the broad categories of disease or infirmity conditions, as summarized in Fig. 3. The architectures for both services are discussed subsequently.

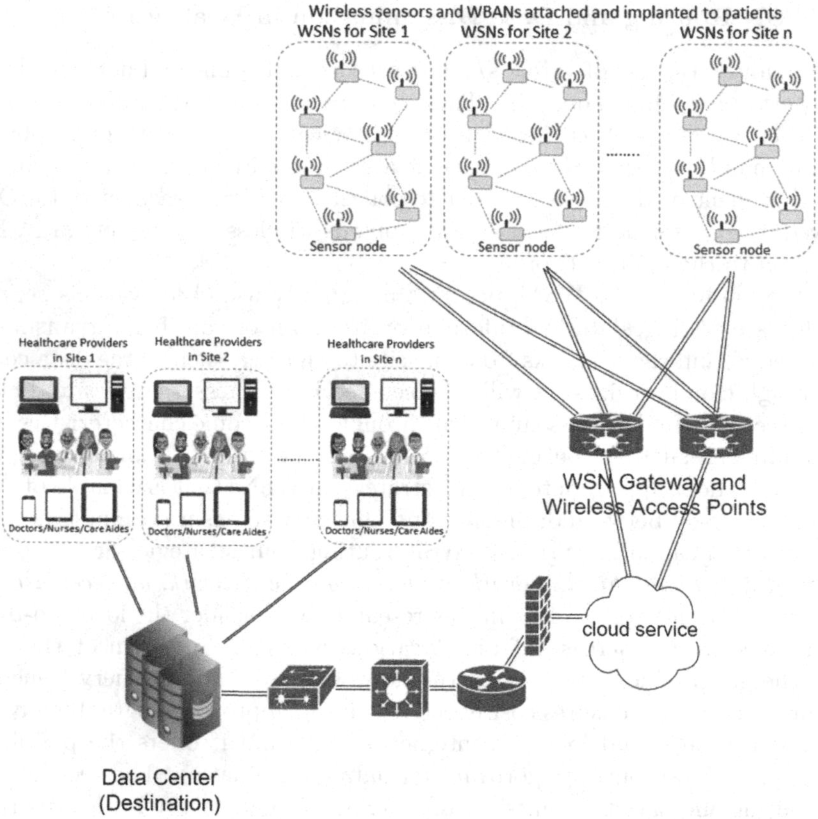

Fig. 2. WSN routing and data transmission.

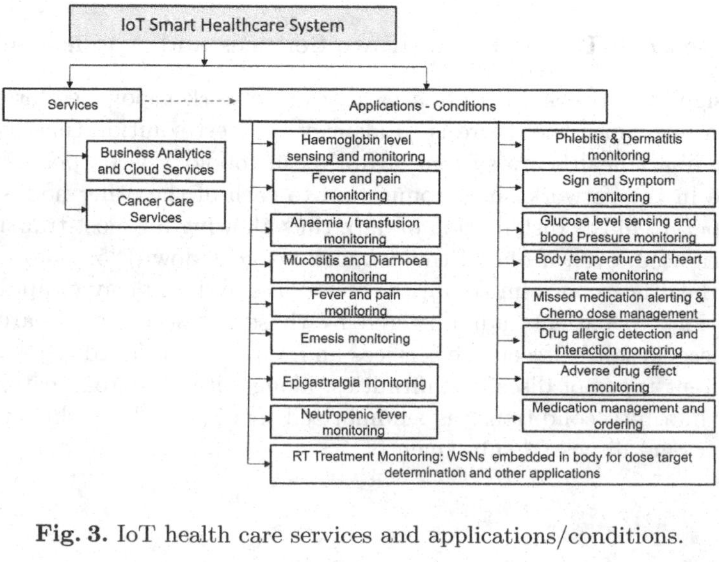

Fig. 3. IoT health care services and applications/conditions.

4 Network Design Solutions for Services

4.1 Cancer Care Services

Essentially, cancer care services comprise of two sub-services associated with the diagnosis and treatment of cancer, namely, chemotherapy and radiotherapy. The chemotherapy is associated with medical oncology (MO) while the radiotherapy (RT) is associated with radiation oncology (RO). The use of smart devices and wireless sensors can be applied towards improving the quality of cancer care services and patient care by seamless and secure integration of those devices in medical oncology and radiation oncology procedures. This is argued in [16] that patient care (i.e. monitoring, alerting, and following-up) for cancer patients undergoing chemotherapy can safely be moved into the home.

As pointed out in [8], attaching and embedding WSNs and smart devices to patients can enhance cancer treatments by allowing health practitioners/nurses to monitor and be alerted of any changes, complications, problems, signs, symptoms, adverse effects, allergies, pains, infections, toxic effects, neutropenic fever occurrences, missed medications, haemoglobin level issues, drug allergic detection, drug interaction, phlebitis, dermatitis, mucositis, diarrhoea, infection of upper respiratory tract, emesis, epigastralgia, neutropenic fever, etc. These issues can automatically be detected, subdued, and blocked, thereby influencing patient care and attention related to patient treatment and enforcing what controls to put in place to circumvent those changes, issues, effects, and symptoms.

Although, [1] claims that no perfect methodology for identifying the magnitude of the adverse effects and issues of chemotherapy, but as alluded by [8], the MO cancer care services can incorporate smart devices that provide assistance to cancer patients in the event of any issues/complications through process automation, remote monitoring, and alert communication. In essence, the IoT technologies through WSNs/smart devices can be programmed at certain level of precision to determine fairly reasonable magnitude deemed fit for the adverse effects of those characteristics on the body. With this innovation, the level of care to patients undergoing such issues can be monitored as shown in Fig. 3.

On the other hand, the implementation of IoT and WSN devices in radiation oncology treatment or radiotherapy is different because of the manner the prescription doses are being administered to patients. Though the use of IoT connected devices can be applied as depicted in Fig. 4. Generally, prior to the DICOM communicating with the various pieces of software, a sequence of steps for the RT treatment starts with the generation of treatment plans in *Eclipse*^{TM} by associating related files, namely computed tomography (CT) files, radiotherapy (RT) structure files and dose-volume as applicable to commercial treatment planning system, *Eclipse*^{TM} with DICOM as interface [6]. This leads to the determination of prescription doses or final dose calculation for the targets or disease sites and the dose volume constraints for organ at risk (OAR). This is followed by the uploading of plan DICOM files back to Eclipse and recalculating the dose and dose volume history (DVHs), then finally doing the evaluation on Eclipse and also conducting patient QA for dosimetric analysis of internal anatomy because emphasis should be placed on the accurate definition for the targets to ensure precision of protons radiotherapy prior to administering of the doses to patients [6]. Having discussed above, we have to admit that the use of inherent smart devices and wireless sensor networks could help achieve intended results for patient treatment. Therefore, the use of IoT technology can be beneficial for administering radiotherapy to patients as it could help improve the margin, preciseness, and accuracy of the radiotherapy doses to ensure they hit the targets/disease sites thereby eliminating geometric uncertainties in setup, patient motion, and patient changes. In this case, WSNs or IoT devices can be implanted or embedded close to the targets, and this will ensure the doses from the linear accelerator do not miss their targets. WSNs are perceived to be useful in achieving better treatment planning results toward appropriate prescription doses.

From Fig. 4, the Health Level-7 (HL7) connectivity utilizes XML technology for interoperating two or more systems for data definition and message exchanging, sharing and reusing within and between lab centres and clinics. On the other hand, the Digital Imaging and Communications in Medicine (DICOM) connectivity communicates with the various pieces of software for transmission of diagnostic images while the embedded systems, such as Laboratory Interface System (LIS), Pathology Interface System (PIS) and Radiology Interface System (RIS), serve as access points for the healthcare providers to access patient information relating to lab results, malignancy or abnormal (pathology) results, and radiology results. In wrapping up, all these systems along with the pharmacy, medical oncology, and radiation oncology servers allow access to comprehensive patient chart information from any device (workstations, tablets, etc.) either at the clinical environment or via remote VPN access from outside the clinic(s). The underlying technologies being considered include: Bluetooth Low Energy (BT-LE), Near Field Communication (NFC), Radio Frequency Identification (RFID), and 6LoWPAN/WiFi/ZigBee [8]. Figure 4 illustrates the network architecture for the proposed cancer care services.

4.2 Business Analytics and Cloud Services

With the growing rate of patient data generated by means of the wireless sensor networks (i.e. WBANs, wearables, smart devices, and embedded systems), data, queries and physical characteristics as observed from these devices and equipment are gathered and collected for researching, analyzing and reporting purposes; gaining intelligence; formulating insights; streamlining operations; and gaining competitive business advantage.

The incorporation of business analytics and cloud services to cancer care services ensures availability and accessibility of patient data being streamed from various sources on a real-time and continuous basis. This, in turn, enables the ever-increasing data to be managed and shared across the healthcare network systems upon deployment into the cloud. Obviously, streams of data are relayed and generated about patients and for some medical devices (through sensors and other connected devices) as related to the patients. These data, in form

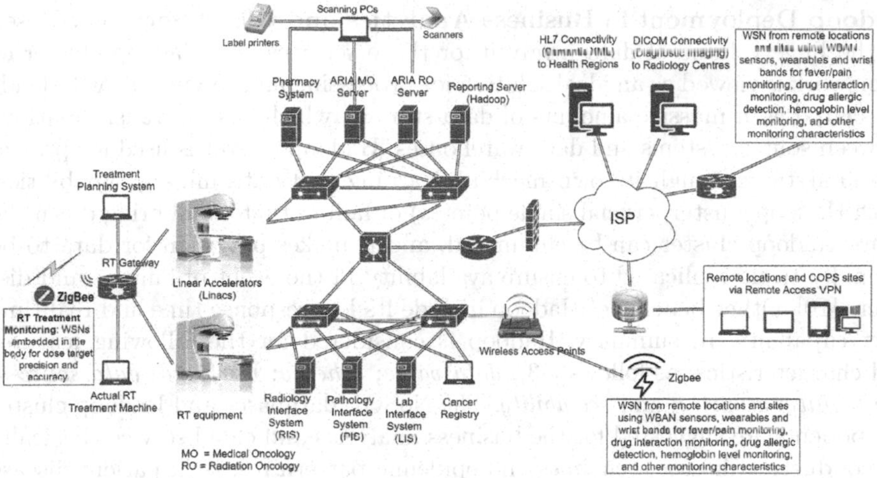

Fig. 4. Cancer care services network architecture.

of multimedia, textual and visual formats, are transmitted through the cloud services to remote servers (data center). As a result, the volume, velocity, and variety of health data and information of patients have continually increased significantly, which puts challenges for analysis and interpretation of data for decision-making purposes using appropriate data analytical tools [8,14].

This architecture also offers reporting capabilities for immediate dashboards that facilitate treatment decisions as we will be able to discover patterns from all the data from various services in order to analyze the quality of care and risk, disease and epidemic pattern, patient/facility monitoring and optimization, etc. This, indeed, will be beneficial to healthcare providers to turn a stream of data into actionable insights and evidence-based healthcare decisions about the health conditions of patients, and also for helping the clinical experts and research groups to keep up to date with the latest trends and breakthroughs in clinical oncology practices. The architecture uses the Picture Archiving Communication System (PACS), which comprises of secure computer systems for storage, retrieval, and display of diagnostic images such as X-rays, CT scans, Magnetic Resonance Imaging (MRIs), etc. The PACS constitutes an important component, where the diagnostic images are being retrieved and accessed through the business analytics and cloud services as made available on the cloud. In view of this, we have proposed an appropriate strategy to gather and analyze data as collected across the network fabric and communications infrastructure through secure transmissions from one end to the other. The details of the network architecture for the business analytics/cloud services are as depicted in Fig. 5, where the initial figure in [8] has been modified to include PACS component.

Hadoop Deployment in Business Analytics and Cloud Services. Based on the huge volume of data involved for those services, the Hadoop cluster or framework is viewed as an ideal solution for processing and solving the workloads associated with massive amounts of data storage, which ensure transformations between source systems and data warehouses. Hadoop cluster is used for predictive analytics through its own machine learning and data mining capabilities. With Hadoop cluster, crucial single point(s) of failure that could bring down the entire Hadoop cluster can be eliminated, and it makes provision for data to be normally triple replicated to ensure availability in the event of failures and disasters [10]. Other benefits of Hadoop include its low response time and real time alert capability. In summary, Hadoop is considered for the following features and characteristics, as follows [13]: *data value*; *schema*; *workload*; *data sources*; *availability*; *security*; and *scalability.* The NoSQL databases and Hadoop cluster components are suggested for the business analytics and cloud services basically for conducting disease, genomics and epidemic pattern research; patient-disease tracking and monitoring; patient sentiment analysis; risk and quality of care analysis; etc. (as shown in Fig. 5).

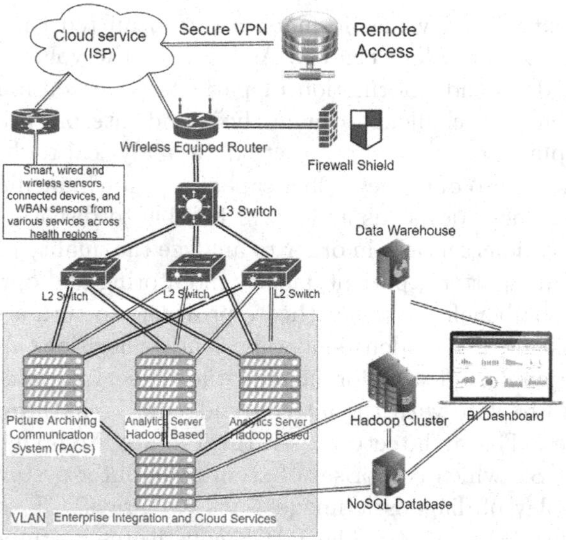

Fig. 5. Business analytics and cloud services network architecture [8].

4.3 Operational Challenges and Security Issues

In [8], we have outlined the analysis of the operational challenges and security issues to cancer care services based on IoT, which we will suggest to the reader to read it though additional information is provided here. While using business analytics on patient data, the issues of confidentiality and privacy have been a concern without exposing the patient demographic information to the research group and business experts. As a result, we will ultimately ensure that patient-sensitive information is protected and encrypted as this may be a major threat and barrier in realizing the potential benefits of business analytics services in healthcare environment, which could deter business improvements, if not addressed.

Since there are various nodes, wireless devices and sensors in the proposed solutions, then we have to ensure that those devices conform to industry standard (i.e. meeting the service- and operational-level agreements) that guarantee reliability and security. In addition, the reliability of the network system is very paramount especially due to the nature of the healthcare environment coupled with the sensitivity of patient information/data. This is one of the reasons why mesh topology is proposed, especially at the distribution layer such that every data transmitted from the source is accepted at the destination within a reasonable time. It is also to ensure high availability with minimal equipment failure and human intervention.

4.4 Securing IoT Services and Devices

Knowing that the security of patient medical data cannot be underestimated and jeopardized, then it becomes imperative to talk about securing the various devices and services being made available during the design of the IoT based medical system in order to avoid leakage of patient information. Hence, some feasible security mechanisms as related to this research include but not limited to: *security for communication in IoT*. For the communication in IoT devices from one layer to another in the network architecture, the three layouts: core, distribution, and access, should be an utmost consideration in terms of security and protection due to the nature of the healthcare environment; *security approaches or mechanisms for WSN, smart connected and remote (RFID) devices*. It is equally paramount to ensure security mechanisms for the WSNs that characterize the IoT solution through securing the routing protocols to prevent attacks that could affect the entire network. In addition, the security mechanisms can be extended to prevent illegal node access, while at the same introduce trust management and distribution mechanism for the WSN routing for data privacy and location privacy of patients within and outside the clinical environment, more so that a large number of nodes is required coupled with the generation/dissemination of a large amount of data; *security for IPv6 (6LoWPAN)*. The use of low power consumption devices and sensors should be considered especially with long-term device or sensory operation coupled with the involvement of human lives (as for devices that are embedded in the human body or with contact with the human body). This will certainly mandate the use of low power IPv6 architecture in the design of the IoT based solution with low power consumption for secured integration; and *security, privacy, and encryption of actuators/sensors, remote devices are equally important*.

5 Conclusions and Future Work

We have proposed the implementation of the IoT based medical system, with reference to cancer care services and business analytics/cloud services, for enhanced treatment, diagnosis, and monitoring of cancer patients. The healthcare solution has been accomplished through the use of WSNs and smart connected devices. This is because WSN plays an important role that allows a number of spatially distributed autonomous sensors to be linked to the network fabric based on geographical routing from source to destination, which facilitate data transmission/exchange. We have also delved into business analytics/cloud services that ensure the availability of patient data stream for actionable insights and evidence-based healthcare decisions. Also addressed are the operational and security challenges associated with the deployment of IoT based medical system due to the nature of the environment and the sensitivity of patient information. This is necessary prior to the go-live phase of the IoT based solution implementation to avoid failure to the entire system and breach of patient data.

In wrapping up, it is worth mentioning that there are various services being delivered in healthcare settings but we have only covered the cancer care and business analytics/cloud services. Hence, we will be considering and integrating more services in our future research work in the same research domain.

References

1. Baena-Canada, J.M., et al.: Use of health-care services during chemotherapy for breast cancer. Eur. J. Cancer **48**, 3328–3334 (2012)
2. Dineshkumar, P., SenthilKumar, R., Sujatha, K., Ponmagal, R.S., Rajavarman, V.N.: Big data analytics of IoT based Health care monitoring system. In: IEEE Uttar Pradesh Section International Conference on Electrical, Computer & Electronics Engineering, pp. 55–60 (2016)
3. Fan, Y.J., Yin, Y.H., Xu, L.D., Zeng, Y., Wu, F.: IoT-based smart rehabilitation system. IEEE Trans. Industr. Inf. **10**(2), 1568–1577 (2014)
4. Lakkis, S., Elshakankiri, M.: IoT based emergency and operational services in medical care systems. In: 13th CTTE/CMI Conference on Internet of Things - Business Models, Users, & Networks, Denmark (2017)
5. Lewis, W.: LAN Switching and Wireless. CCNA Exploration Companion Guide. Cisco Press, Indianapolis (2009)
6. Liu, W.: Robustness quantification and worst-case robust optimization in intensity-modulated proton therapy. In: Rath, A.K., Sahoo, N. (eds.) Particle Radiotherapy, pp. 139–155. Springer, New Delhi (2016). https://doi.org/10.1007/978-81-322-2622-2_10
7. Lu, D., Liu, T.: The application of IoT in medical system. In: IEEE International Symposium on IT in Medicine and Education, vol. 1, pp. 272–275 (2011)
8. Onasanya, A., Elshakankiri, M.: IoT implementation for cancer care & business analytics/cloud services. In: Proceedings of the 10th IEEE/ACM International Conference on Utility & Cloud Computing (UCC 2017), pp. 205–206, Austin, TX, (2017). https://doi.org/10.1145/3147213.3149217

9. Rahmani, A., Thanigaivelan, N.K., Gia, T.N., Granados, J., Negash, B., Liljeberg, P., Tenhunen, H.: Smart e-health gateway: bringing intelligence to internet-of-things based ubiquitous healthcare systems. In: 12th Annual IEEE Consumer Communications and Networking Conference (CCNC), pp. 826–834 (2015)
10. Riazul Islam, S.M., Kwak, D., Kabir, H., Hossain, M., Kwak, K.S.: The IoT for health care: a comprehensive survey. IEEE Access **3**, 678–708 (2015)
11. Satija, U., Ramkumar, B., Sabarimalai Manikandan, M.: Real-time signal quality-aware ECG telemetry system for iot-based health care monitoring. IEEE Internet Things J. **4**(3), 815–823 (2017)
12. Sohraby, K., Minoli, D., Znati, T.: Wireless Sensor Networks: Technology, Protocols, & Applications. John Wiley & Sons Inc., NJ (2007)
13. Stackowiak, R., Licht, A., Mantha, V., Nagode, L.: Big Data and The IoT. Enterprise Information Architecture for A New Age. Apress, Ontario (2015)
14. Yao, J.T., Onasanya, A.: Recent development of rough computing: a scientometrics view. In: Wang, G., et al. (eds.) Thriving Rough Sets, Studies in Computational Intelligence, vol. 708, pp. 21–45 (2017)
15. A Wireless Sensor Networks Bibliography. Autonomous Networks Research Group. http://ceng.usc.edu/~anrg/SensorNetBib.html#0103. Accessed 25 May 2017
16. IoT project for home cancer care. http://wireless.electronicspecifier.com/around-the-industry/internet-of-things-project-for-home-cancer-care. Accessed 5 June 2017
17. State of IoT Healthcare by Aruba, an HP Enterprise company. http://www.arubanetworks.com/iot. Accessed 25 May 2017

Privacy Preserving for Location-Based IoT Services

Yue Qiu(✉) and Maode Ma

School of Electrical and Electronic Engineering,
Nanyang Technological University, Singapore, Singapore
QIUY0005@e.ntu.edu.sg, emdma@ntu.edu.sg

Abstract. In recent years, the applications of location-based Internet of Things (IoT) services change the way of people's lives and works. However, these applications may disclose some private location information of users due to lack of privacy protection mechanism, which could result in serious security issues. To protect users' confidential data, an efficient and secure private proximity testing (ESPT) scheme is designed for location-based IoT services to improve the efficiency while maintaining the privacy of the location of the users. The proposed scheme enables a user to query a service provider whether some people are within a given search range without disclosing any private location information of the user. The security analysis and the simulation results demonstrate that the proposed scheme could not only implement a privacy-preserving proximity test, but also has less computational overheads.

Keywords: Bloom filter · Location privacy · Proximity testing Security

1 Introduction

In recent years, smartphones, tablets and other wearable devices have become ubiquitous due to rapid development of electronic industry. Internet of Things (IoT), which is going to connect everything in the world, has provided an infrastructure to connect those mobile devices to make people be able to access various wireless network services at anytime and anywhere. Among various network services, location-based service (LBS) has attracted considerable attention, which can be applied into various areas of human life such as social networking applications, healthcare services, financial services and etc. Users' locations are the key enabler of the LBS and can be easily measured by various mobile IoT devices using Global Positioning System (GPS). With the locations information of users, the LBS could provide more valuable services, such as private proximity test, which enables a user to get the information whether some people are within a given geometric range.

Although the LBS is a promising application in IoT and can offer more precise and valuable services based on the location information of users, it should be cautiously used due to privacy concerns [1, 2]. However, most of the applications require users to

A.-S. K. Pathan et al. (Eds.): SGIoT 2018, LNICST 256, pp. 36–45, 2019.
https://doi.org/10.1007/978-3-030-05928-6_4

upload their current locations through different IoT devices without strong privacy protection. The leakage of the private location information of users may be maliciously taken to track users, which could lead to severe consequences.

Motivated by the above-mentioned privacy concerns, many privacy-preserving proximity tests have been proposed to protect users' locations. A private proximity test using private equality testing (PET) and location tags has been proposed in [3]. To improve the efficiency, a vectorial private equality testing (VPET) with an untrusted server has been proposed based on linear algebra in [4]. Another privacy-preserving proximity test with an untrusted server using ElGamal encryption has been proposed in [5] to allow users to verify the correctness of test result instead of a LBS server. A private proximity based location sharing scheme, named Near-pri, using Paillier encryption has been proposed in [6] to allow users to maintain their own security policy. Compared to Near-pri, a more efficient and privacy-preserving proximity testing with differential privacy techniques (EPPD) has been proposed in [7]. Two schemes to support location based handshakes and private proximity testing with location tags using Bloom filter and Bose-Chaudhuri-Hocquenghem (BCH) code have been proposed in [8, 9]. While most schemes only support one coordinate system, a privacy-preserving distance computation and proximity testing has been proposed to support three different coordinate systems on earth in [10]. Although the above-mentioned proximity testing can protect the information of users' locations, most of them only supports proximity testing between two parties, which may result in a high computational overhead when deployed in the real world.

In this paper, as our major contribution, an efficient and secure private proximity testing (ESPT) with location tags is proposed for location-based IoT applications to improve the efficiency while maintaining privacy of the location information of users. The users' location information uploaded to an untrusted third party will be protected by differential privacy techniques for the LBS [7, 11]. The private proximity testing is performed based on the cloaking location tags, a Bloom filter [12] and a secure dot product protocol [13] without disclosing users' confidential data to adversaries. The security functionality of the proposal is evaluated by formal verification and its efficiency is demonstrated by the simulation results. It can be shown that the ESPT scheme could not only preserve privacy, but also incur less computational overhead.

The remainder of this paper is organized as follows. In Sect. 2, the system model is introduced. In Sect. 3, the proposed scheme is described in details. The security analysis and the performance evaluation of the proposed scheme is presented in Sect. 4. Finally, the paper is concluded in Sect. 5.

2 System Model

The system model under this study is shown in Fig. 1, including many registered users, a service provider and a trusted authority.

- User: Each user should be registered before accessing the services. After registration, the registered users need to periodically upload the information of their current locations through mobile IoT devices. The location information is encrypted and stored in the service provider's database. A user can initiate a request for searching other users within a fixed search area by using the proposed ESPT scheme.
- Service Provider (SP): The service provider is responsible for storing users' encrypted location information and providing secure proximity testing based on users' locations and search range. The SP is an honest-but-curious entity, which means that although it operates through the defined steps of the protocol, it may be curious about the private information of locations of the users.
- Trusted Authority (TA): The TA, which is responsible for system initialization and assigning key materials to registered users and the SP, is fully trusted by other entities.

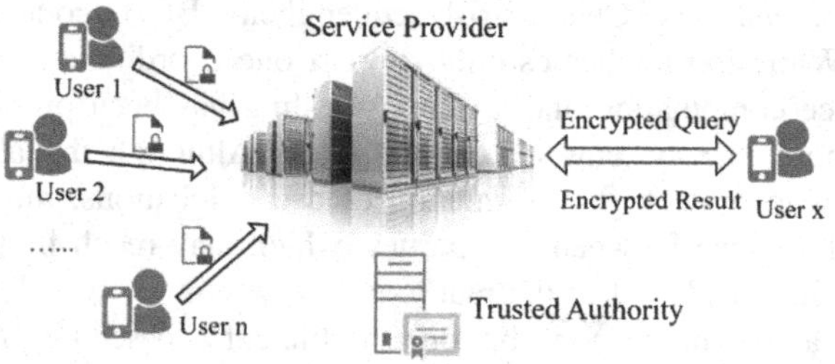

Fig. 1. The system model

3 Proposed ESPT Scheme

In this section, based on differential privacy techniques for location-based services [7, 11] including a bloom filter [12] and a secure dot product protocol [13], an efficient and secure private proximity testing (ESPT) scheme is proposed. It consists of three phases: system initialization phase, user location uploading phase and privacy-preserving proximity testing phase.

3.1 System Initialization Phase

Before accessing the services provided by the SP, the TA is responsible for generating public parameters and assigning keys to the users and the SP in the following steps:

- Given a security parameter k_1, a large prime p is selected, such that $|p| = k_1$. A cyclic group G of prime order p, in which the discrete logarithm problem (DLP) is hard, is generated. The TA also generates a random generator $h \in G$ and chooses hash functions $H : \{0, 1\}^* \rightarrow G$.

- Given the parameter $\epsilon \in \mathbb{R}^+$, the TA transfers the map into a map with many grids. The side length μ of a grid depends on the privacy level used by the system. When the side length becomes longer, the privacy level increases. Each grid has a grid tag, such as $tag1_{i,j} = (i,j)$ and each grid is divided into several small grids. The side length of them is l and area tag is $tag2_{i',j'} = (i',j')$ as shown in Fig. 2. The location (x,y) of a user can be mapped into a tag as $tag_{User} = \left(tag1_{i,j}, tag2_{i',j'}\right)$.
- The TA assigns identities to each registered user and the SP, and publishes a parameter list <G, h, p, H, μ, l, ϵ> and area information. Based on the public parameters, the SP selects a random number $sk_{SP} \in \mathbb{Z}_p^*$ as a private key and compute $pk_{SP} = h^{sk_{SP}} mod\, p$. as the corresponding public key. Each user U_i chooses a private key $sk_i \in \mathbb{Z}_p^*$ and computes $pk_i = h^{sk_i} mod\, p$ as his public key.

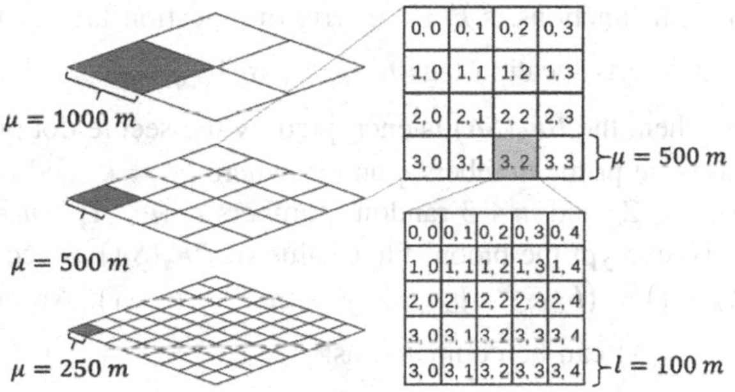

Fig. 2. Grid maps and location tags

3.2 User Location Uploading Phase

Before uploading the location information of the users to the SP, the users need to convert their GPS locations into the form of xy-coordinates in the Cartesian plane by the Miller Projection, which is similar as the procedure in the EPPD scheme in [7]. To protect the information of the current locations of users from being tracking by the adversaries, each user $U_i \in U$ periodically uploads his/her cloaking location data to the SP. The detailed steps of the user location uploading phase are described as follows.

- According to geo-indistinguishability [11], U_i computes a cloaking location coordinates (cx_i, cy_i) based on U_i's current location coordinates (x_i, y_i) as $cx_i = x_i + r\cos\theta$ and $cy_i = y_i + r\sin\theta$, where $r = -\frac{1}{\epsilon}\left(W_{-1}\left(\frac{p-1}{e}\right) + 1\right)$, $\theta \in [0, 2\pi)$ and $p \in [0,1)$. After that, U_i maps his/her current location (x_i, y_i) into area tags $tag_x = \left(tag1_{i,j}, tag2_{i',j'}\right)$, and maps the cloaking location (cx_i, cy_i) into a cloaking location tag $ctag1_{U_i}$.
- U_i calculates a symmetric key established with the SP as $k_{i \leftrightarrow SP} = H\left(pk_{SP}^{sk_i} \| ID_{SP} \| ID_i \| H(tsp)\right)$, where tsp is a timestamp. The cloaking tag is encrypted as $CT_i = ENC_{k_{i \leftrightarrow SP}}(ctag1_{U_i} \| ID_{SP} \| ID_i \| tsp)$ and will be sent to the SP in the message <$CT_i \| ID_i \| tsp$>.

- Upon receiving the uploaded location tag from a user, the SP checks the timestamp and calculates the symmetric key $k_{SP \leftrightarrow i} = H\left(pk_i^{sk_{SP}} \| ID_{SP} \| ID_i \| H(tsp)\right)$. CT_i can be successfully decrypted if $k_{SP \leftrightarrow i}$ is correctly computed. The SP stores the information <$ctag1_{U_i}, ID_i, tsp$> in its database which will be further used in the private proximity testing.

3.3 Private Proximity Testing Phase

During the private proximity testing phase, a user U_x sends a test request to the SP including the location tag and a search area. The detailed steps are described as follows.

- Step 1: If a user U_x would like to perform a private proximity testing, U_x needs to set a search area SA which can be a rectangle area or an arbitrary area which consists of different location tags. Then, a bloom filter is generated with the length of m, and the number of hash functions is k. U_x inserts the location tags to the bloom filter within the SA. It inserts location tags $tag_x = \left(tag1_{xi,xj}, tag2_{xi',xj'}\right)$ into $BF_x(SA) = \left(b_{x,1}, \ldots, b_{x,m}\right)$. Then, the $BF_x(SA)$ is encrypted by the secure dot product protocol. U_x chooses two large prime numbers q and α, where $|q| = k_2$ and $|\alpha| = k_3$. A large random number $s \in Z_q$ and $m+3$ random numbers c_i $(i = 1, .., m+3)$ with $|c_i| = k_4$ are chosen. To encrypt the bloom filter value of $BF_x(SA)$, a vector is created as $\overrightarrow{u_x} = (BF_x(SA), -1) = \left(b_{x,1}, \ldots, b_{x,m}, -1\right) = (u_1, \ldots, u_{m+1})$. An encrypted vector $\overrightarrow{C_x} = (C_1, \ldots, C_{m+3})$ can be computed as:

$$C_i = \begin{cases} s(u_i \cdot \alpha + c_i) \bmod p, & u_i \neq 0 \\ s \cdot c_i \bmod p, & u_i = 0 \end{cases} \quad (1)$$

  for each element $u_i (i = 1, \ldots, m+3)$, where $u_{m+2} = u_{m+3} = 0$. The cloaking search area SA' centered at the $ctag1_{U_x}$ is sent to the SP, which can be the same size as the real search area or bigger than it. U_x computes a session key as $k_{x \leftrightarrow SP} = H\left(pk_{SP}^{sk_x} \| ID_{SP} \| ID_i \| H(tsp_x)\right)$, encrypts the vector as $CT_x = ENC_{k_{x \leftrightarrow SP}} \left(H\left(q \| \alpha \| \overrightarrow{C_x}\right) \| ID_{SP} \| ID_x \| SA' \| tsp_x\right)$, and sends the test request <$q \| \alpha \| \overrightarrow{C_x} \| CT_x \| ID_{SP} \| ID_x \| SA' \| tsp_x$> to the SP and keep $s^{-1} \bmod q$ secret.
- Step 2: When receiving the request from U_x, the SP first checks if the time interval is below the defined threshold using the timestamp tsp_x and the current time. The SP also computes the session key as $k_{SP \leftrightarrow x} = H\left(pk_x^{sk_{SP}} \| ID_{SP} \| ID_x \| (tsp_x)\right)$, decrypts the received ciphertext as $DEC_{k_{SP \leftrightarrow x}}(CT_x) = H\left(q \| \alpha \| \overrightarrow{C_x}\right) \| ID_{SP} \| ID_i \| SA' \| tsp_x$ and validates the hash value using the received information. According to the U_x's uploaded location tag $ctag_{U_x}$, the SP sends the encrypted vector $\overrightarrow{C_x}$, q and α to users U^* whose location area is within or intersects the search area SA', and users whose location tags are neighbors to U^*, as shown in Fig. 3.

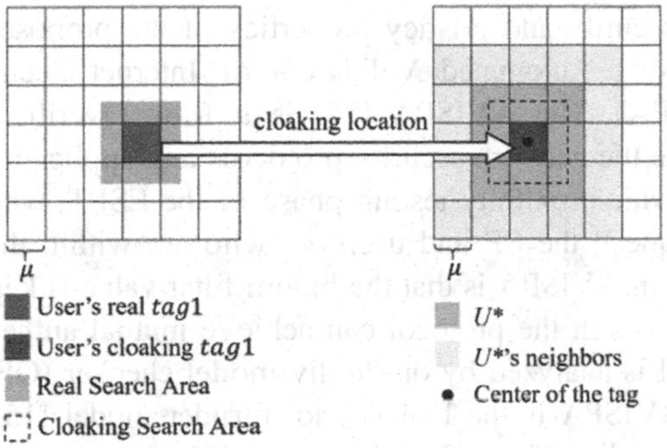

Fig. 3. Private proximity test

- Step 3: When the user U_y receives the $\overrightarrow{C_x}$, U_y creates a bloom filter with the length and the hash functions to be same as $BF_x(SA)$. The location tag $tag_y = \left(tag_{yi,yj}, tag_{yi',yj'}\right)$ is the only element inserted into the bloom filter $BF_y(tag_y)$. To calculate the dot product, a vector is created as $\overrightarrow{v_y} = (BF_y(tag_y), k) = (b_{y,1}, \ldots, b_{y,m}, k) = (v_1, \ldots, v_{m+1})$. U_y compyutes a encrypted vector $\overrightarrow{D_y}$ based on the $\overrightarrow{C_x}$ as:

$$D_i = \begin{cases} v_i \cdot \alpha \cdot C_i \, mod \, q, & v_i \neq 0 \\ r_i \cdot C_i \, mod \, q, & v_i = 0 \end{cases} \tag{2}$$

for each element $v_i (i = 1, \ldots, m+3)$, where r_i ($|r_i| = k_5$) is a random number, and $v_{m+2} = v_{m+3} = 0$. After that, U_y calculates the sum of D_i as $D_y = \sum_{i=1}^{m+3} D_i \, mod \, p$, and sends a message $<D_y \| CT_y \| ID_{SP} \| ID_y \| tsp_y>$ to the SP, where $CT_y = ENC_{k_{y \leftrightarrow SP}}(H(D_y) \| ID_{SP} \| ID_y \| tsp_y)$ and the session key $k_{y \leftrightarrow SP} = H\left(pk_{SP}^{sk_y} \| ID_{SP} \| ID_y \| H(tsp_y)\right)$.
- Step 4: After receiving all the response messages, the SP sends a result message $<D_1 \| \ldots \| D_n \| ID_1 \| \ldots \| ID_n \| CT_{SP} \| ID_{SP} \| ID_x \| tsp_{SP}>$ to U_x, where $CT_{SP} = ENC_{k_{SP \leftrightarrow x}}(H(D_1 \| \ldots \| D_n \| ID_1 \| \ldots \| ID_n) \| ID_{SP} \| ID_x \| tsp_{SP})$ and a session key $k_{SP \leftrightarrow x} = H(pk_x^{sk_{SP}} \| ID_{SP} \| ID_x \| H(tsp_{SP}))$.
- Step 5: U_x computes the session key $k_{x \leftrightarrow SP} = H(pk_{SP}^{sk_x} \| ID_{SP} \| ID_x \| H(tsp_{SP}))$ to decrypt the message from the SP. After successfully obtaining $D_1, \ldots, D_n$, U_x tries to exract the dot products by using $\overrightarrow{u_x} \cdot \overrightarrow{v_j} = \sum_{i=1}^{m+3} (u_{xi} \cdot v_{ji}) = \frac{E_{xj} - (E_{xj} mod \, \alpha^2)}{\alpha^2}$, where $E_{xj} = s^{-1} \cdot D_j mod \, p$ $(1 \le j \le n)$. If $\overrightarrow{u_x} \cdot \overrightarrow{v_j} = 0$, U_j is within the real search area SA.

4 Security and Performance Evaluation

In this section, the security and privacy properties of the proposed ESPT scheme is analyzed first by using Automated Validation of Internet Security Protocols and Applications (AVISPA). The AVISPA [14] is a formal verification tool that can automatically validate the network security protocols and applications. There are three basic roles in the private proximity testing phase of the ESPT, which are the user U_x who sends a test request, the SP and users U_i who are within the search area. The security goal defined in AVISPA is that the bloom filter value is kept secret during the test, and the participants in the protocol can achieve mutual authentication. The proposed ESPT protocol is analyzed by on-the-fly model checker (OFMC). The intruder model used in the AVISPA is the Dolev-Yao intruder model [15, 16]. The intruder initially has all the public information, its own public/private key pair and its own identity. As shown in Fig. 4, the output result demonstrates that the ESPT is safe under the goals as specified.

```
SUMMARY
  SAFE
DETAILS
  BOUNDED_NUMBER_OF_SESSIONS
PROTOCOL
  /Users/apple/Downloads/span/testsuite/results/epst.if
GOAL as specified
BACKEND OFMC
STATISTICS
  TIME 210 ms
  parseTime 0 ms
  visitedNodes: 128 nodes
  depth: 6 plies
```

Fig. 4. AVISPA result

Then, the computational overhead is analyzed by JAVA and conducted on Intel(R) Core(TM) i7-4790 CPU @ 3.60 GHz, 16 GB Ram, Windows 7 (64-bit). The applied cryptographic algorithms employed in the simulations are hash function, Secure Hash Algorithm-256 (SHA-256), and Advanced Encryption Standard-Cipher Block Chaining-256 (AES-CBC-256). In our simulations, users are uniformly deployed in an area of 20 km $*$ 20 km. The parameters used in the simulations are $\epsilon = 2$, $\mu = 500$, $l = 100$, $k_1 = 1024$, $k_2 = 512$, $k_3 = 200$, $k_4 = 128$, and $k_5 = 128$.

To compare the efficiency of our proposed ESPT scheme with the EPPD scheme, the average computational cost in the user location uploading phase with different numbers of users is presented in Fig. 5(a). The EPPD scheme needs to calculate and upload the cloaking coordinate of each user while the ESPT scheme only uploads the

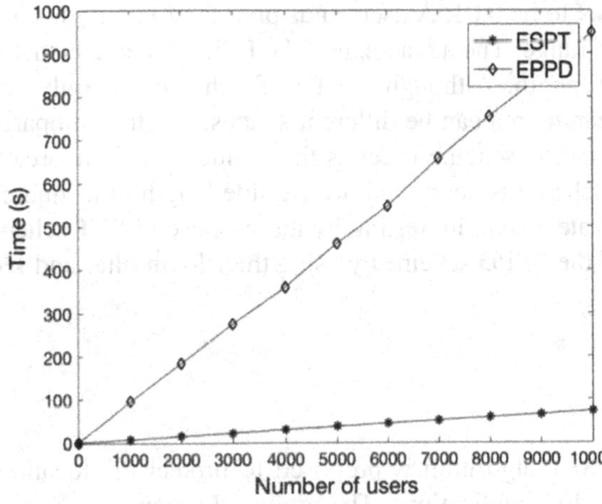

(a). Average Computation Cost of User Location Uploading Phase

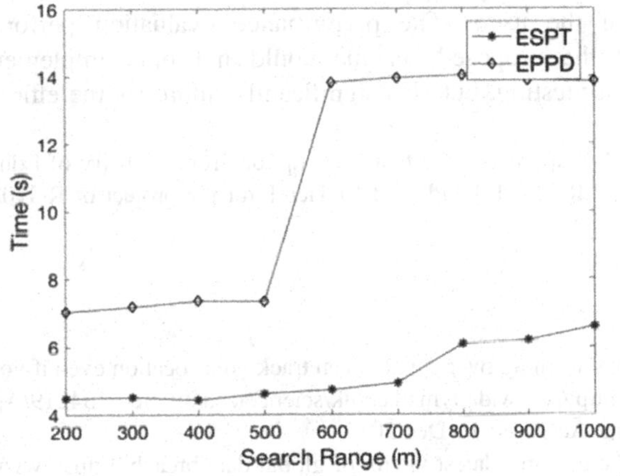

(b). Average Computation Cost of a Private Proximity Test

Fig. 5. Performance evaluation

users' location tag to the SP, which can largely save the computational time in the location uploading process. The average computational time of a single user by the ESPT scheme is about 7.27 ms, which shows that the ESPT scheme is more efficient than the EPPD scheme.

If the size of the Bloom filter is fixed, the number of false positives is proportional to the number of data inserted. To save the computational time, the size of the Bloom Filter m is dynamic with a given probability of false positives p in the ESPT scheme, which can be computed as $m = -\frac{n \ln p}{(\ln p)^2}$, and the number of hash functions k is computed as $k = -\log_2 p$, where n is the number of inserted elements. In the private proximity testing phase, the total number of users is set to 10000 and the probability of false positives p is set to be 0.01. A user sends private proximity test requests to the SP with different search range. The advantage of the EPPD scheme is that the search radius can be an arbitrary length. Although the ESPT scheme can only search in units of location tags, the search area can be different shapes. For the comparison purpose, the search range of the EPPD scheme is set as the radius of a circle area while the search range of the ESPT scheme is nearly half of the side length of a square area. As shown in Fig. 5(b), the private proximity testing by the proposed ESPT scheme is much more efficient than that of the EPPD scheme by using the Bloom filter and secure dot product protocol.

5 Conclusion

In this paper, the ESPT algorithm is proposed to protect the location information of users for the LBS of IoT applications. The proposed scheme enables a user to query a SP whether some persons are within a given search range without any location privacy disclosure. The security analysis proves that the ESPT scheme can preserve location privacy for all of the users. The performance evaluation performed by JAVA demonstrates that the proposed scheme could not only implement the privacy-preserving proximity testing, but also significantly improves the efficiency.

Acknowledgment. We appreciate the financial support from Ministry of Education, Singapore through the Academic Research Fund (AcRF) Tier 1 for the project of RG20/15.

References

1. Prigg, M.: Privacy warning over app that can track your location even if you turn GPS off on your phone. http://www.dailymail.co.uk/sciencetech/article-5134219/App-track-location-turn-GPSoff.html. Accessed 10 Dec 2017
2. Chong, Z.: Obike becomes latest victim of global data breach. https://www.cnet.com/news/yellow-bike-sharing-firm-is-new-victim-of-global-data-breach/. Accessed 12 Dec 2017
3. Narayanan, A., Thiagarajan, N., Lakhani, M., Hamburg, M., Boneh, D.: Location privacy via private proximity testing. In: Proceedings of NDSS 2011 (2011)
4. Saldamli, G., Chow, R., Jin, H., Knijnenburg, B.P.: Private proximity testing with an untrusted server. In: Proceedings of 6th ACM Conference on Security and Privacy in Wireless and Mobile Networks 2013, WISEC 2013, pp. 113–118. ACM (2013)
5. Zhuo, G., Jia, Q., Guo, L., Li, M., Fang, Y.: Privacy-preserving verifiable proximity test for location-based services. In: Proceedings of IEEE Global Communications Conference 2015 (GLOBECOM 2015), pp. 1–6. IEEE, USA (2015)
6. Novak, E., Li, Q.: Near-PRI: private, proximity based location sharing. In: Proceedings of IEEE INFOCOM 2014, pp. 37–45. IEEE, Canada (2014)
7. Huang, C., Lu, R., Zhu, H., Shao, J., Alamer, A., Lin, X.: EPPD: efficient and privacy-preserving proximity testing with differential privacy techniques. In: Proceedings of IEEE International Conference on Communications 2016 (ICC 2016), pp. 1–6. EEE, Malaysia (2016)

8. Zheng, Y., Li, M., Lou, W., Hou, Y.T.: SHARP: private proximity test and secure handshake with cheat-proof location tags. In: Foresti, S., Yung, M., Martinelli, F. (eds.) ESORICS 2012. LNCS, vol. 7459, pp. 361–378. Springer, Heidelberg (2012). https://doi.org/10.1007/978-3-642-33167-1_21
9. Zheng, Y., Li, M., Lou, W., Hou, Y.T.: Location based handshake and private proximity test with location tags. IEEE Trans. Dependable Secure Comput. **14**(4), 406–419 (2017)
10. Sedenka, J., Gasti, P.: Privacy-preserving distance computation and proximity testing on earth, done right. In: Proceedings of the 9th ACM Symposium on Information, Computer and Communications Security 2014 (ASIA CCS 2014), pp. 99–110 (2014)
11. Andr´es, M.E., Bordenabe, N.E., Chatzikokolakis, K., Palamidessi, C.: Geo-indistinguishability: differential privacy for location-based systems. In: Proceedings of the 2013 ACM SIGSAC Conference on Computer & Communications Security (CCS 2013), pp. 901–914 (2013)
12. Wang, B., Li, M., Wang, H.: Geometric range search on encrypted spatial data. IEEE Trans. Inf. Forensics Secur. **11**(4), 704–719 (2016)
13. Lu, R., Zhu, H., Liu, X., Liu, J.K., Shao, J.: Toward efficient and privacy-preserving computing in big data era. IEEE Netw. **28**(4), 46–50 (2014)
14. The AVISPA Team: AVISPA v1.1 User Manual. http://www.avispa-project.org/package/user-manual.pdf. Accessed 21 Aug 2017
15. Viganò, L.: Automated security protocol analysis with the AVISPA tool. Electron. Notes Theoret. Comput. Sci. **155**, 61–86 (2006)
16. Dolev, D., Yao, A.: On the security of public key protocols. IEEE Trans. Inf. Theory **29**(2), 198–208 (1983)

Smart Home Security Application Enabled by IoT:
Using Arduino, Raspberry Pi, NodeJS, and MongoDB

Chad Davidson[1], Tahsin Rezwana[2], and Mohammad A. Hoque[2](✉)

[1] Department of Electrical Engineering and Computer Science, University of Tennessee Knoxville, Knoxville, TN 37996, USA
cdavid11@vols.utk.edu

[2] Department of Computing, East Tennessee State University, Johnson City, TN 37614, USA
{rezwana,hoquem}@etsu.edu

Abstract. Recent advances in smartphones and affordable open-source hardware platforms have enabled the development of low-cost architectures for IoT-enabled home automation and security systems. These systems usually consist of a sensing and actuating layer that is made up of sensors such as PIR (Passive Infra-red) sensors, also known as motion sensors; temperature sensors; smoke sensors, and web cameras for security surveillance. These sensors, smart electrical appliances and other IoT devices connect to the Internet through a home gateway. This paper lays out architecture for a cost effective "smart" door sensor that will inform a user through an Android application, of door open events in a house or office environment. The proposed architecture uses an Arduino-compatible Elegoo Mega 2560 microcontroller (MCU) board along with the Raspberry Pi 2 board for communicating with a web server that implements a RESTful API. Several programming languages are used in the implementation and further applications of the door sensor are discussed as well as some of its shortcomings such as possible interference from other RF (Radio Frequency) devices.

Keywords: Smart home · Security · IoT · Arduino · Raspberry Pi NodeJS · MongDB · RF transmission

1 Introduction

Smart home is a section of the Internet of Things (IoT) paradigm that aims to integrate home automation and security. Enabling objects in a typical household to be connected to the Internet allows home-owners to remotely monitor and control them. From lamps that are set on timers to turn off at a specific time of the day, to smart thermostats that will regulate the temperatures in a house and generate detailed reports about energy usage, smart homes have found it's

A.-S. K. Pathan et al. (Eds.): SGIoT 2018, LNICST 256, pp. 46–56, 2019.
https://doi.org/10.1007/978-3-030-05928-6_5

niche in the consumer market. The availability of affordable smartphones, microcontrollers and other open-source hardware along with the increasing use of cloud services, has made it possible to develop low-cost smart home security systems. With families having busier lives than ever, smart home automation and security systems can also cater to household members with limited mobility such as the handicapped and the old.

The purpose of this paper is to present a low-cost architecture using RF based communication in a household to create an IoT-enabled smart home security system. Smart home devices that typically consume low power such as smart bulbs and door or window sensors use RF transceivers to communicate with each other. In this paper, an inexpensive architecture is proposed for a smart door sensor that will utilize an Elegoo Mega 2560 microcontroller board, Raspberry Pi 2, a web server, and an Android application.

2 Related Work

Prior work in IoT-enabled home security system has proposed architectures that focused on the use of low-cost open-source hardware components like the Arduino and Raspberry Pi MCU boards and a combination of sensors. PIR (Passive Infrared) sensors are used to detect motion and can work in sync with a webcam that captures images to alert users of trespassing.

Kodali et al. describe a cost-effective wireless home security and automation system based on the TI-CC3200 LaunchPad: a battery-powered microcontroller unit (MCU) with built-in WiFi connectivity [1]. PIR motion sensors are placed at the entrances to a building and connect to a digital in-out pin of the MCU. The MCU is programmed using Energia IDE (Integrated Development Environment) and Wi-Fi enabled. Kodali et al.'s configuration allows mobile phones without Internet connectivity to receive security alerts and control IoT devices connected to the microcontroller. Tanwar et al. describe an inexpensive home security system that implements a real-time email alert system [2]. The system uses a PIR module and a Raspberry Pi MCU. Security cameras and PIR sensors are connected to the Raspberry Pi via USB ports and GPIO (General Purpose Input/Output) pins respectively. The system assumes that homes have Internet access; it uses the Internet to send e-mails to the resident in real-time. The system's intrusion detection logic identifies motion by comparing signal inputs from the PIR sensors with their previous values. When current and previous signals differ, the security camera captures an image that is stored temporarily on the Raspberry Pi and then automatically e-mailed to the resident.

Gupta and Chhabra describe a cost-effective Ethernet-based smart home system for monitoring energy consumption, smoke and temperature levels and detecting trespassing [3]. This system uses the Arduino-certified Intel Galileo 2nd generation microcontroller board. Temperature, smoke and PIR sensors are connected directly to the microcontroller, while four 220 V devices are connected via a relay module. An android based mobile app that connects to the Intel Galileo based server over the Internet allows users to toggle switching devices by tap-to-touch or voice commands through Google API speech recognition tools.

Piyare et al. present a Bluetooth-based home automation system where an Android cell phone running a Python script communicates with an Arduino BT board with digital and analog input/output ports to which sensors and appliances are connected [4]. The smartphone application has a toggle on and off feature for each device. However, Bluetooth connectivity between the smartphone and the Arduino BT board required a range of 50 meters or less within a concrete building and mobile platforms other than Symbian do not support the Pyhton application.

Behera et al. designed and implemented a real-time smart home automation system using an Arduino Uno board along with an Arduino Wi-Fi Shield and a PC home server [5]. A PIR or motion sensor, an LDR (Light Dependent Resistor) and an LM35 temperature sensor were used to collect data which was made available on the PC server that also implemented a MATLAB-GUI platform to control the temperature, lights, and fans. The PIR sensor also acted as a security component by detecting possible intrusions and setting off a buzzer to alert the residents.

Howedi et al. proposed a low-cost smart home system built upon a similar architecture using the Arduino Uno board, PIR sensors, DHT11 temperature sensors, INA219 high side DC current sensor and servo motors that control doors and windows [6]. The Arduino IDE is used to implement the control and monitoring module of the system while the MIT App Inventor is used to develop a simple Android application.

Panwar et al. implemented the Eyrie smart home automation system using the Raspberry Pi 3 MCU as the central hub [7]. Their proposed architecture connected several Arduino Nano boards located around the house to various types of sensors and NRF24L trans-receivers that eliminated the need for Ethernet or Wi-Fi connectivity. Mosquito Broker, an open-source message broker used for relaying messages to the Raspberry Pi 3, operates using the Debian OS. Eclipse SmartHome framework was used to implement a web interface and a smartphone app for end-users.

In [8], a home automation system with smart task scheduling is developed making use of wireless ZigBee to connect appliances and wired X10 technology to connect light and switch modules to an Arduino microcontroller. An Ethernet shield mounted on the Arduino MCU allows communication between Arduino and a Web-based Android application which is then used to remotely add and manage devices and view recommended scheduling.

ShariqSuhail et al. implemented a prototype for smart home security system that uses PIR sensors for intrusion detection, MQ2 sensors for detecting smoke and gas leaks, LM35 temperature sensors as input to an Arduino Mega 2560 [9]. A buzzer, LCD, LED strip and a GSM module are outputs to this MCU board while a Raspberry Pi 2 board is used to include a webcam that captures images upon motion detection. GSM (Global System for Mobile communication), a wireless technology interfaces with the Arduino Mega to send SMS notifications and calls to the user's cell phone whenever potential intrusion, smoke or gas leak is detected.

In [10], a similar architecture utilizes an Arduino Mega 2560 board with a Wi-Fi module to implement a voice-controlled smart home system. The Elechouse V3 voice recognition module allows users to send voice commands to adjust lighting, open or close windows and control a folding bed.

Vineeth's et al. voice-controlled secure eHome also make use of the V3 voice recognition module but use an RF module instead of Wi-Fi for wireless communication between an Arduino UNO and Raspberry Pi MCUs [11]. The Raspberry Pi supports sensor connectivity to the Internet so all sensory data can be logged onto a Google spreadsheet. There is no implementation of a mobile or web app thus confining the controlling of this system to the location of the mic.

Sunehra et al. propose two schemes for a speech-based home automation system [12]. The first scheme uses HC-05 Bluetooth module along with Arduino Bluetooth controller mobile application to control appliances when inside the house. GSM/GPRS technology is used to remotely control appliances and receive SMS alerts for possible intrusion detections. The ARM11 Raspberry Pi board acts as the central hub for receiving voice commands though the HC-05 Bluetooth module and connects to a PIR sensor, relays, a Wi-Fi router and a webcam.

3 System Architecture and Design

3.1 Devices and Sensors

- Elegoo Mega 2560 Board (or Arduino)
- RF Receiver-Transmitter Pair (433 Hz)
- Magnetic Reed Switch
- Raspberry Pi 2
- Female to Female-Female to Male Jumper Cables
- Android phone or emulator

3.2 Schematics

Figures 1 and 2 describe the schematics for wiring the Elegoo Mega and Raspberry Pi boards. In Fig. 1, a magnetic reed switch and RF 433 Hz transmitter is attached to the Mega 2560 board. The ordering of the wires do not matter for the reed switch. One wire leads to ground and for the code located in the repository, pin 2 on the Mega 2560 board is where the other wire will lead. The RF transmitter has leads to ground, a 5 V power supply, and a lead to pin 10 on our board. The antenna used for this project is a simple rolled piece of aluminum foil.

Figure 2 presents a diagram of the pinout of the Raspberry Pi 2 attached to an RF Receiver. The RF Receiver has leads to ground, a 5 V power supply, and to pin 13 on the Raspberry Pi (used in OpenDoor.cpp in repository). Note that there is a second Data pin that is not to be utilized in this project and an antenna (not pictured) was formed out of rolled aluminum foil.

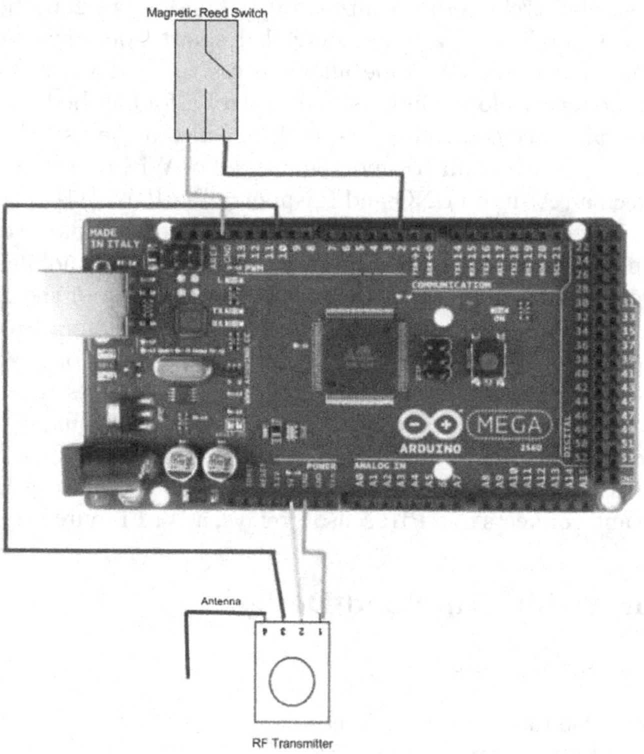

Fig. 1. Mega 2560 board with magnetic reed switch and RF transmitter diagram

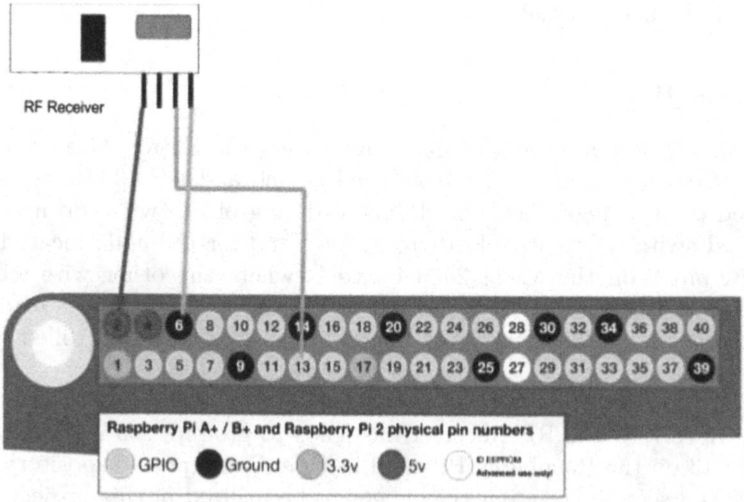

Fig. 2. Raspberry Pi-2 pinout diagram with RF Receiver Wiring

3.3 System Architecture

Figure 3 describes the overall architecture of the smart home security system. Figure 4 shows the flow diagram of data communication. Each of the following subsections provide a detailed explanation of how the devices communicate with each other. A simple overview of the system architecture will help understand why the sections have been laid out in the order they are. Initially, the reed switch is opened which causes the Elegoo board to send an RF signal from its transmitter to the RF receiver located on the Raspberry Pi 2. The Raspberry Pi then sends an HTTP POST request to a RESTful web server that is set up in the cloud. This web server then either pushes information, or receives GET requests from an Android application to allow the end user to view the door open events by date and time. All libraries mentioned in the following sections are open source.

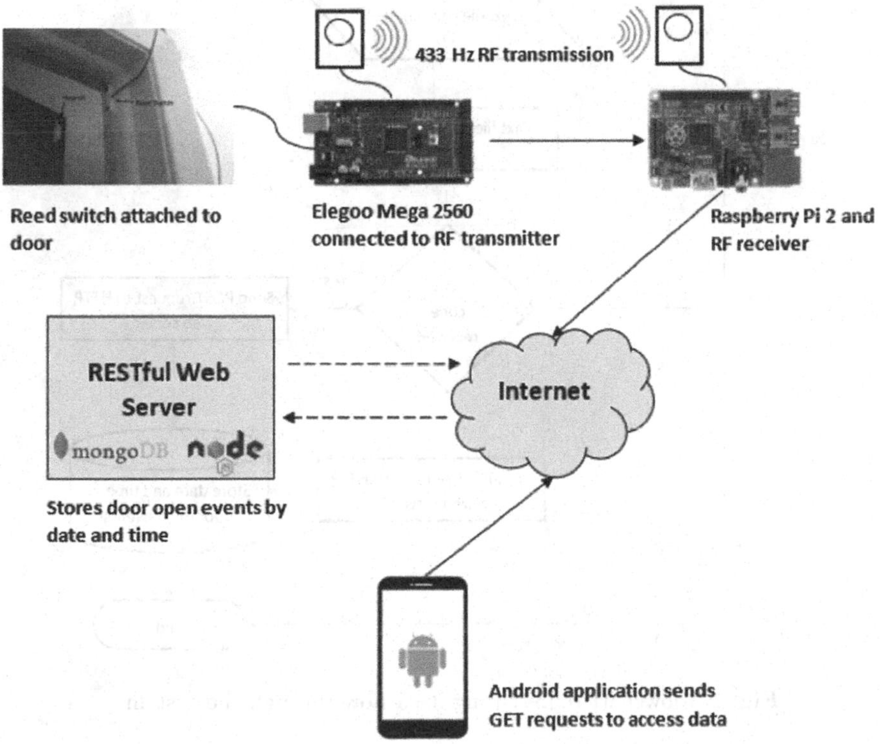

Fig. 3. System architecture for IoT-based smart home security

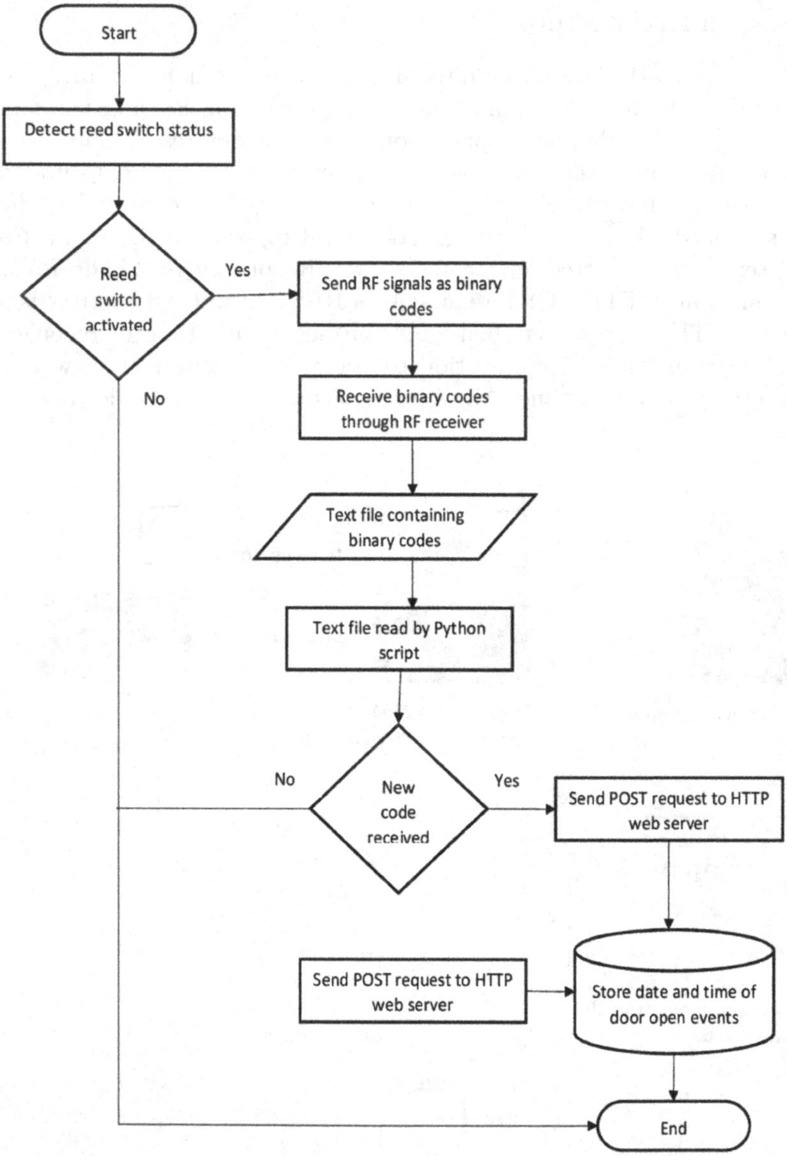

Fig. 4. Flowchart representing data flow through the system.

3.4 Communication Between Elegoo and Raspberry Pi-2

The connection between the Elegoo and the Raspberry Pi is the most important part as it is where the sensor in the IoT architecture communicates with another device. Once the door is open and the reed switch is activated, an RF transmission of 433 Hz is sent from the transmitter using the rc-switch library for the

Arduino. A binary code is sent to the receiver connected to the Raspberry Pi and it is incremented for every subsequent door open event. This enables the Raspberry Pi to keep track of individual door open events. The RF transmission range was tested in a 1200 sq. ft apartment. When the reed switch is activated, a constant stream of binary numbers is transmitted to the receiver attached to the Raspberry Pi. Using a simple piece of aluminum foil as antennae on the receiver and the transmitter, the entire 1200 sq. footage of the house is covered. The Raspberry Pi utilized the wiringPi library and the 433Utils library to receive the binary codes. These codes are then sent as a text file output that is read by a Python script that will perform the next step of the communication process.

3.5 Communication Between Raspberry Pi-2 and NodeJS Web Server

When the binary codes have been received and sent as output to a text file, a Python script utilizing the Requests library checks the text file every second for new updates. When a new code is placed in the text file, a POST request is then sent to an HTTP web server that is set up with NodeJS and a MongoDB database. This server implements a RESTful API that stores door open events by date and time. The data located in this database are accessible via GET requests that can be performed by the Android application.

3.6 Communication Between Web Server and Android Device

The final step in the communication process is between the web server and the Android application written in Java. It is possible to send push notifications whenever a new door open event is detected by the web server, however, for the purposes of this project, the Android application makes GET requests to the server. The Android application uses a variety of libraries that are available through the Android Studio but the library used to make the requests is the Volley library.

4 Future Scope

This design can be used as a reference for further applications to be developed with the current sensor architecture, and it provides a framework using the Raspberry Pi through which other sensors can be added to the smart home network.

4.1 Reed Switch Applications

The door sensor provides a way of seeing whether or not a door has been opened. The most obvious way to extend this application is to record the amount of time a door is open. While this may be useful to individual end users, there lies a possible business interest in knowing how often the doors to a store are opened and closed. This information can then be used by businesses to lower their energy costs.

A second future application for this architecture could include connecting a Bluetooth module to the Mega 2560 board to identify individuals entering through the door by pairing with an end users phone. It could also be used by parents to check on a child that may try to leave home at an odd hour.

4.2 Further Raspberry Pi Applications

Since the Raspberry Pi uses an RF receiver it can not only receive the transmission from the magnetic reed switch but also be outfitted with the ability to receive transmissions from other RF-enabled devices in the household. The Raspberry Pi could be used as a hub for RF-enabled smart home devices throughout the house. The concept can be used to develop a more advanced home security system that would include PIR motion sensors placed in other areas of the house to detect intrusion while homeowners are away. Using, RF-enabled bulbs the smart home system can be extended to include energy management inside the house.

The Raspberry Pi can serve as a fog computing device which can store information locally before sending it to the cloud server. This can be useful when applications might need real time support or low latency that cannot be provided by the cloud service.

4.3 Android Application Improvements

The Android application for this project, written in Java, is a basic application. Future work may involve adding time zone support from the device so as not to depend solely on Unix timestamps. Multiple options to view and display the data located in the MongoDB database, can also be added. A calendar feature can be integrated so users can have a more robust view of the door open events in their household. The system can be enhanced to display alerts to users in the form of SMS or email in the event of trespassing.

5 Limitations

Potential issues may arise through interference on the 433 Hz RF frequency. Many home devices use RF signals to communicate and at a given time there may be more than one RF receiver trying to send signals to the Raspberry Pi or it could be picking up signals that it wasn't intended to receive. An interference testing with the RF units can be done as a part of future work. In the case of multiple transmitters attempting to communicate with the Raspberry Pi, there would need to be a registration system in place on the Raspberry Pi that kept track of incoming signals and their sources. However, the architecture proposed here does not provide that support.

6 Conclusion

This paper presents an architecture that can be used as framework to build a low-cost smart home security system. Using affordable components such as microcontrollers from Elegoo and Raspberry Pi and RF signals as a communication channel between these devices, it was possible to develop an IoT system that allows users of a household to view when a particular door has been opened. Schematics for connecting the different components have been provided along with figures to demonstrate them. The data flow between each of these devices have been explained and potential issues that may arise have been discussed. Finally, future work in this area along with potential use cases for this architecture have also been discussed.

References

1. Kodali, R.K., Jain, V., Bose, S., Boppana, L.: IoT based smart security and home automation system. In: 2016 International Conference on Computing, Communication and Automation (ICCCA), pp. 1286–1289. IEEE, April 2016
2. Tanwar, S., Patel, P., Patel, K., Tyagi, S., Kumar, N., Obaidat, M.S.: An advanced Internet of Thing based security alert system for smart home. In: 2017 International Conference on Computer, Information and Telecommunication Systems (CITS), pp. 25–29. IEEE, July 2017
3. Gupta, P., Chhabra, J.: IoT based Smart Home design using power and security management. In: 2016 International Conference on Innovation and Challenges in Cyber Security (ICICCS-INBUSH). IEEE (2016)
4. Piyare, R., Tazil, M.: Bluetooth based home automation system using cell phone. In: 2011 IEEE 15th International Symposium on Consumer Electronics (ISCE), pp. 192–195. IEEE, June 2011
5. Behera, A.R., Devi, J., Mishra, D.S.: A comparative study and implementation of real time home automation system. In: 2015 International Conference on Energy Systems and Applications, pp. 28–33. IEEE, October 2015
6. Howedi, A., Jwaid, A.: Design and implementation prototype of a smart house system at low cost and multi-functional. In: Future Technologies Conference (FTC), pp. 876–884. IEEE, December 2016
7. Panwar, A., Singh, A., Kumawat, R., Jaidka, S., Garg, K.: Eyrie smart home automation using Internet of Things. In: Computing Conference, 2017, pp. 1368–1370. IEEE, July 2017
8. Baraka, K., Ghobril, M., Malek, S., Kanj, R., Kayssi, A.: Low cost arduino/android-based energy-efficient home automation system with smart task scheduling. In: 2013 Fifth International Conference on Computational Intelligence, Communication Systems and Networks (CICSyN), pp. 296–301. IEEE, June 2013
9. ShariqSuhail, M., ViswanathaReddy, G., Rambabu, G., DharmaSavarni, C.V.R., Mittal, V.K.: Multi-functional secured smart home. In: 2016 International Conference on Advances in Computing, Communications and Informatics (ICACCI), pp. 2629–2634. IEEE (2016)
10. Gunputh, S., Murdan, A.P., Oree, V.: Design and implementation of a low-cost Arduino-based smart home system. In: 2017 IEEE 9th International Conference on Communication Software and Networks (ICCSN), pp. 1491–1495. IEEE, May 2017

11. Vineeth, K.S., Vamshi, B., Mittal, V.K.: Wireless voice-controlled multi-functional secure ehome. In: 2017 International Conference on Advances in Computing, Communications and Informatics (ICACCI), pp. 2235–2240. IEEE, September 2017
12. Sunehra, D., Tejaswi, V.: Implementation of speech based home automation system using Bluetooth and GSM. In: 2016 International Conference on Signal Processing, Communication, Power and Embedded System (SCOPES), pp. 807–813. IEEE, October 2016

An MQTT-Based Scalable Architecture for Remote Monitoring and Control of Large-Scale Solar Photovoltaic Systems

Salsabeel Shapsough(✉), Mohannad Takrouri, Rached Dhaouadi, and Imran Zualkernan

American University of Sharjah, Sharjah, UAE
salsabeelshapsough@gmail.com

Abstract. This paper presents a novel IoT-based architecture that utilizes IoT communication, software, and hardware technologies to enable real-time monitoring and management of solar photovoltaic systems at a large scale. The system enables stakeholders to remotely control and monitor the photovoltaic systems and evaluate the effect of various environmental factors such as humidity, temperature, and dust. The system was implemented and evaluated in terms of network delay and resource consumption. MQTT demonstrated an average network delay of less than 1 s, proving the architecture to be ideal for solar and smart grid monitoring systems. At the hardware, the evaluation showed the hardware to consume about 3% of the panel's capacity, while the application also utilized a very small percentage of the CPU. This lead to the conclusion that the proposed architecture is best deployed using low-cost constrained edge devices where a combination of efficient MQTT communication and low resources consumption makes the system cost-effective and scalable.

Keywords: IoT · Solar photovoltaic monitoring

1 Introduction

Studying the effect of dust and other atmospheric conditions on remote solar photovoltaic systems has been recognized as key to more efficient solar power generation. While soiling, especially the accumulation of dust particles on panels, is known to reduce solar panel efficiency [1], the cost of periodic cleaning can somtimes exceed the cost ensued by dust accumulation [2]. It is therefore important to monitor the PV panels soiling level to optimize the cost of cleaning, especially as the scale increases from few solar panels to solar farms. Similar challenges also exist with other environmental factors such as haze, moisture, and temperature [3, 4]. Furthermore, the tilt angle of a solar panel array can influence the solar radiance harnessed by the panel PV [5]. Controlling the angle, therefore, can not only maximize the power output, but also assist in building a model that predicts the optimal solar array installation in a specific region. Thus, the ability to remotely monitor and control multiple solar farms has since been recognized to hold the key to optimum solar power generation.

A.-S. K. Pathan et al. (Eds.): SGIoT 2018, LNICST 256, pp. 57–67, 2019.

1.1 Background

Several designs for solar photovoltaic remote monitoring systems have been previously proposed [6]. A noticeable recent trend in the field has been the adoption of Internet of Things (IoT) concepts and technologies [7] for building such systems. An IoT system consists of numerous, geographically spread nodes that interact with their surroundings, and send information back to a server periodically, based on a certain event, or both. Information is either provided to stakeholders in real-time or stored to be available on demand. The scale of such systems enabled by emergence of new software and hardware technologies that cater for low-cost, scalability, reliability, and security.

1.2 The Internet of Things Paradigm

A generic Internet of Things system consists of five layers: perception, network, middleware, application, and business. In a solar PV system, the perception layer is represented by sensing and actuating elements at the panel level, while the network layer is represented by the wireless intranetworking within a solar farm, and the internetworking between solar farms, remote servers, and stakeholders. The middleware layer hosts technologies responsible for translating raw data into intelligible information, as well as storage and dissemination of information. The application and business layers represent interested stakeholders. While interfaces used by clients and researchers fall under the application layer, operations such as billing and integration with smart grid represent the business layer.

1.3 IoT-Aided Solar Monitoring

The value that IoT technologies can bring to remote monitoring of Solar PV systems has been recognized. Several works have suggested the incorporation of IoT elements in the field. Most such proposals cater to the edge of the IoT system, low-cost edge sensing and processing technologies such as Raspberry Pi, Arduino, BeagleBones, and others are used to acquire readings related to solar panel's power generation efficiency, as well as the surrounding environment [8–10]. Edge devices often act as nodes in mesh networks, connected by short-range wireless technologies such as ZigBee and Bluetooth. One shortcoming of the proposed systems is that beyond the edge, large-scale operations such as dissemination and management of data across the whole system are still performed either by classic internet technologies which are ill-suited for this purpose [11]. In this paper, we present a novel architecture for scalable, almost-real-time monitoring of Solar PV systems, based on a complete IoT paradigm that integrates IoT technologies across the system.

2 Proposed Architecture

The proposed IoT-based architecture is shown in Fig. 1. The edge device at each panel represents the perception element. Each device is equipped with sensors and actuators and is capable of data processing and wireless communication. Data is transmitted wirelessly to reduce cabling costs. Wireless communication can be provided either by an access point that every group of edge devices can connect to over WiFi, Bluetooth, ZigBee, or Thread, or by connecting a 3G/4G module to each individual edge device.

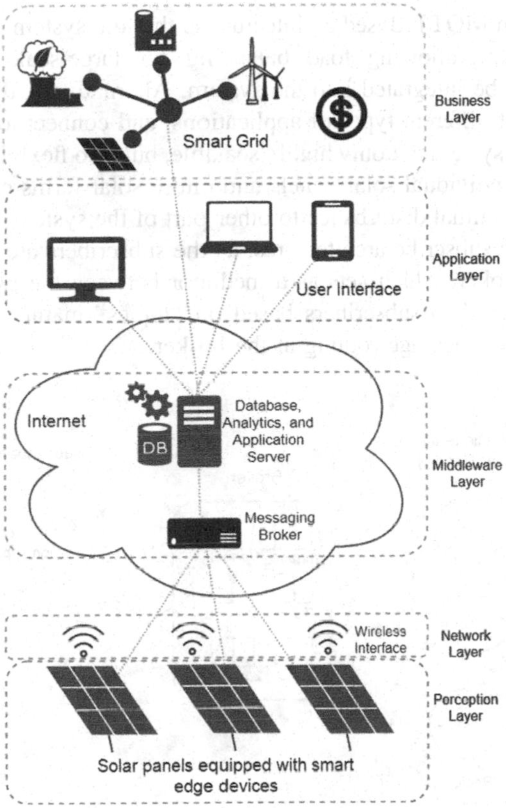

Fig. 1. System architecture

2.1 System Architecture

The first key middleware element is a messaging broker that supports a publish/subscribe communication protocol like Message Queuing Telemetry Transport (MQTT). As opposed to the HypterText Transfer Protocol (HTTP), -which operates in a one-to-one client-request/server-response architecture, MQTT allows event-based, one-to-many, many-to-one, and many-to-many messaging between remote nodes [12]. MQTT also consumes less computational and network resources, while also causing less latency [13]. This makes the protocol an ideal choice for deployment on low-resources edge devices in applications like solar monitoring. The broker keeps a register of subscribed nodes in order to route any new messages from publishers to their correct destinations. In the case of a node going down due to technical issues, the broker retains messages until the node is available again. Other middleware elements are: an application server to manage data and provide a web interface for users, a database to store data, and an analytics engine.

2.2 Communication Architecture

The key aspect of an MQTT-Based architecture is that the system supports the option of distributed servers, allowing load balancing for large-scale systems as more resources can easily be integrated into the system. Alternatively, different servers can be developed to host different types of applications, and connect to different analytics engines, making the system not only highly scalable, but also flexible. On the other end of the architecture, individual solar panels and entire solar farms can easily be added and removed with minimal disturbance to other part of the system. This is yet another advantage of publish/subscribe architectures, as the subscribers are separated from the publishers by the broker, which acts as a mediator between the two. Messages from publishers are delivered to subscribers based on "topics" maintained by the broker. Figure 2 demonstrates message routing at the broker.

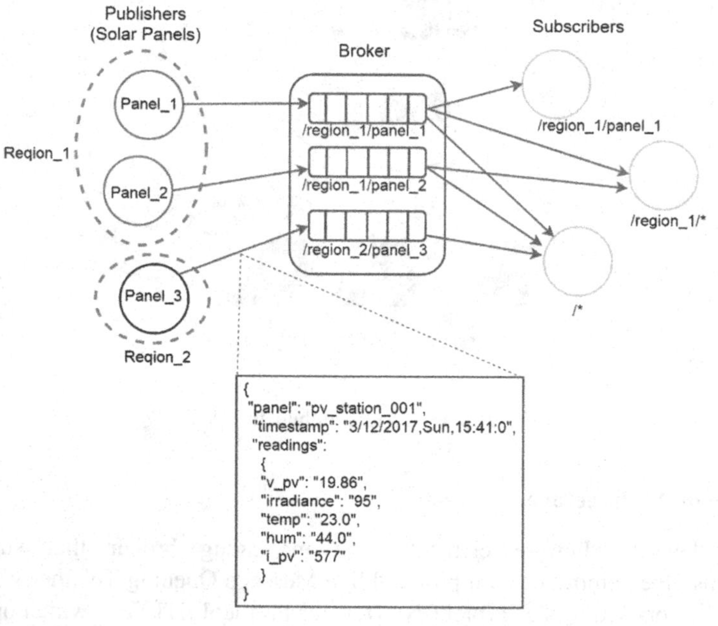

Fig. 2. Communication architecture

Every published message includes a topic following the format of a URL. For example, a PV panel located in "Region 1" of the solar farm and identified by the panel ID "Panel 1" tags its messages with "/region_1/topic_1". Subscribers can choose to subscribe to any topic by sending a one-time subscription request. Subscribers can subscribe to one panel (/region_1/panel_1), all panels in a region (/region_1/*), or all panels in the system (/*). The "*" character acts as a wildcard and allows subscribers to subscribe to numerous publishers with a single request. It is also possible for multiple panels to publish to one topic, e.g. "region_1/dust", or for subscribers to subscribe to sensor-related topics, e.g. "/*/dust". This enables subscribers interested in certain information, such as dust accumulation, for example, to receive updates any new panels added to the system, without the need to pre-register the panel at the subscribers.

2.3 Proof of Concept

Hardware Implementation. As proof of concept, a prototype of the system including hardware and software has been implemented and tested over the past few months. Two types of WiFi-connected Raspberry Pi-based edge stations were designed, implemented, and evaluated. The first type is "pv station", which is a station that is attached to and monitors an individual solar panel. The pv station is equipped with a combination of sensors and actuators to provide different types of monitoring and control. The second type, "c station", is equipped with a Raspberry Pi camera for surveillance. It is also possible to use the videos from the "c station" to perform image processing for research on weather and soiling effect on solar panels. The internal temperature of the Raspberry Pi in all stations is also monitored for troubleshooting. A description of each station's features is shown in Table 1, while the PV stations are shown in Fig. 3.

Table 1. Edge nodes

	C station	PV station 1	PV station 2	PV station 3
Purpose	CCTV	Solar irradiance and PV output monitoring	Solar irradiance and weather monitoring	PV output monitoring and IV characteristics measurement
Main components	• RPi Camera • RPi internal temperature sensor	• Pyranometer • 3 voltage sensors • 3 current sensors • RPi internal temperature sensor	• Pyranometer • Ambient temperature sensor • Humidity sensor • RPi internal temperature sensor	• 2 isolated voltage + current sensors • Temperature sensor • Relay modules • RPi internal temperature sensor
Report frequency	1/minute	1/second	1/minute	1/second
Data type	Video stream	text	text	text
Average packet size		508 Bytes	189 Bytes	346 Bytes

The two pv stations are self-sufficient in terms of power in that the batteries that powers the stations are charged using the solar panel each station monitors. The c station, on the other hand, is powered through a wall socket. Communication between edge

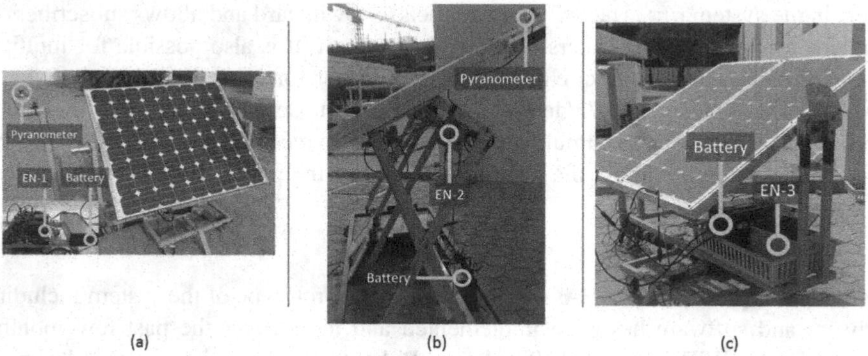

Fig. 3. Edge stations: (a) PV station 1, (b) PV station 2, (c) PV station 3

stations and the rest of the system is carried out over WiFi, while c station is connected via Ethernet to improve video streaming quality.

Backend and Web Application Server. The backend server is the main subscriber to real-time readings. The server was built using NodeJS and Express and is hosted on Amazon Web Services (AWS) which provides a mix of a Platform as a Service (PaaS) and Infrastructure as a Service (IaaS). Readings are stored into DynamoDB, which is a document-based NoSQL database. The main server's Express interface exposes four main functionalities: a standalone solar irradiance interface (Fig. 4), a real-time monitoring, control, and surveillance interface for individual panels (Figs. 5 and 7), a history interface that allows access to archived data logs from specific dates and times (Fig. 6), and an analytics interface. Access privilege levels can range from casual users who can only view the real-time solar irradiance, to high level administrators who are authorized to send control commands to the panels, view analytics, and access the surveillance camera.

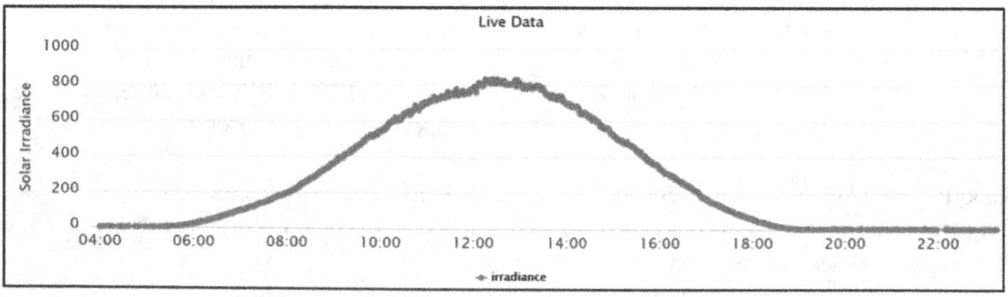

Fig. 4. Solar irradiance over a full day

The importance of the surveillance camera comes from enabling administrators to compare measured values to actual real-time footage. For example, an irregularity was previously noticed in solar irradiance data at around 08:45 am where the irradiance value experiences a sudden jump. Reviewing the surveillance video (Fig. 7) revealed

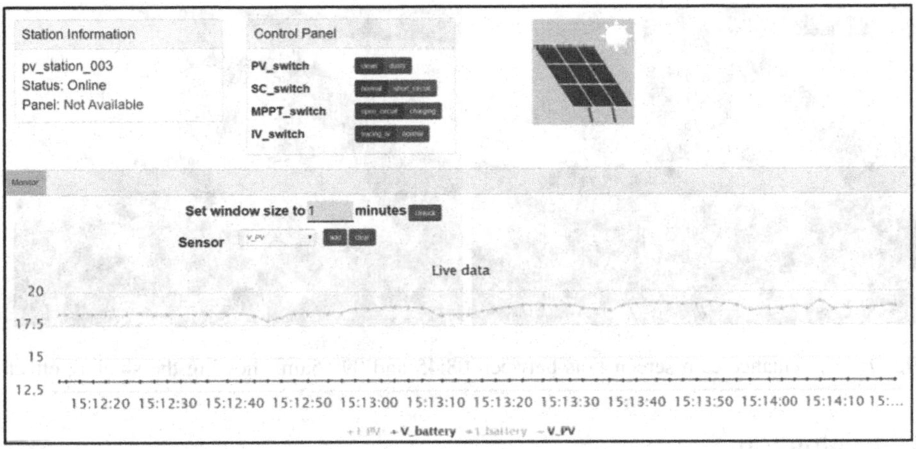

Fig. 5. Real-time interface for PV station 2 showing humidity and temperature

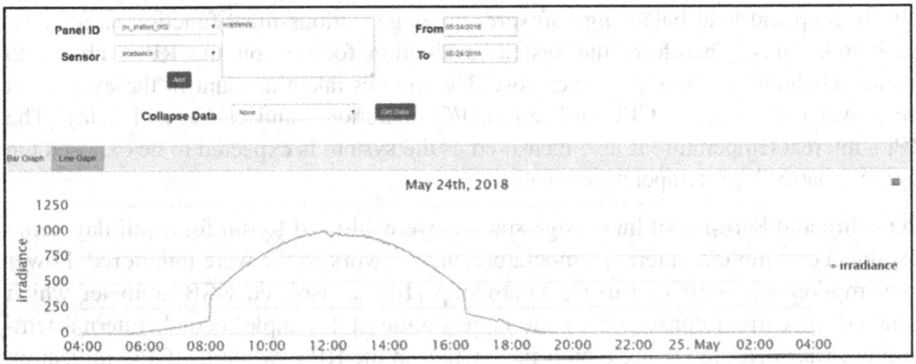

Fig. 6. History interface showing solar irradiance readings log from PV station 2 on May 24th, 2018

that the shading was due to the sun rising from behind the neighboring buildings. Furthermore, the stored footage provides visual data that can be used along with image processing and machine learning algorithms to perform various studies to predict soiling levels and study its effect on the solar power output.

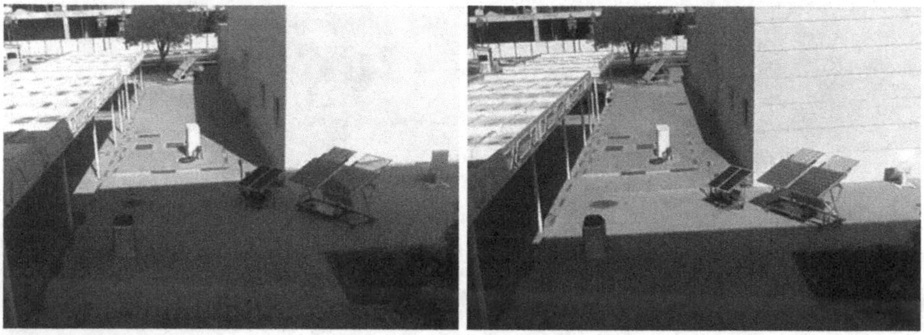

Fig. 7. Surveillance cam screenshots between 08:45 and 09:15am, showing the shading effect

3 Evaluation

The edge stations are the most important elements in the system, yet they have the highest constraints in terms of resources. While the backend server can easily be scaled with backup and load balancing software, the edge stations must function as reliable, standalone units. Therefore, the system evaluation focuses on the RPi's ability to ensure reliability at a low resources cost. The metrics taken account in the evaluation are power consumption, CPU utilization, I/O operations, and end-to-end delay. The RPi's internal temperature is also measured as the system is expected to be exposed the region's harsh, high-temperature weather.

Experimental Setup. All three edge stations were allowed to run for a full day while resource consumption, internal temperature, and network traffic were monitored. Power consumption was measured using YoctoAmp [14], an isolated USB ammeter which sampled the current consumed by the edge station at 1 sample/second. Internal temperature was measured using a built-in function in the RPis, while the CPU utilization and network write rate was measured using the Linux-based performance monitoring tool NMON [15]. The internal temperature was taken at a rate of 1 sample/minute, while the CPU utilization was measured at a rate of 1 sample/second. This is primarily due to the fact that while CPU utilization can change significantly within seconds, the internal temperature remains relatively stable and changes more slowly. Finally, the network end-to-end delay was defined as the time needed for an MQTT packet to travel from the publisher (edge station) to a subscriber and was measured by assigning timestamps at the times of sending and receiving. In order to ensure the accuracy of the end-to-end delay measurement, the clocks of the publisher and the subscriber had to be perfectly synchronized. One way to achieve this is to use the same edge station as the subscriber to its own packets. However, in order to completely avoid the extra subscriber process affecting other metrics such as the CPU utilization and power, the network delay experiments were run separately. The stations were connected to 100-Watt solar panels.

Results. The main findings of the experiment are shown in Table 2. As expected, the station that consumed the highest amount of resources was the camera station.

Compared to the other station, continuous video streaming over WiFi utilizes the CPU by about 60% more and consumes around 50% more power. As for the PV stations, which are the main components of the system, the two stations demonstrate similar consumption of resources. The first conclusion that can be drawn is that the report frequency has insignificant effect on the resource consumption: as the performance is similar despite a difference of a factor of 60 between the sampling frequencies of the two PV stations. Secondly, the low percentage of CPU consumption and the relatively-high power consumption (which amounts to a little under 3% of the solar panel's output) suggest that the stations may not need a device as powerful as the RPi at all. Consequently, the suggested architecture can be improved based on WiFi-enabled microcontrollers with a fraction of the computational power such as an ESP or a smaller Arduino-based microcontroller, thus reducing the cost of hardware and power consumption, while maintaining the same level of reliability. Finally, since the overall goal is to eventually integrate the solar park into a smart grid system, the system latency was compared to general delay requirements in smart grid applications reviewed in [16], which was approximated to be 1 s. The low end-to-end delay proves MQTTS to be well-suited for secure, real-time communication for such a system.

Table 2. Experimental findings

Metric		C station	PV station 2	PV station 3
Power consumption	# of samples	3600	3600	3600
	Mean	3.142 W	2.237 W	2.148 W
	Stdv.	0.165	0.0730	0.0518
Raspberry Pi CPU utilization	# of samples	3600	3600	3600
	Mean	4.824%	2.931%	2.708%
	Min	2.1%	0%	0.3%
	Max	16.2%	15.8%	28%
Raspberry Pi internal temp	# of samples	1440	1440	1440
	Mean	58.475 °C	56.464 °C	51.120 °C
	Stdv.	6.277	6.509	2.156
Network write rate	# of samples	3600	3600	3600
	Mean	245.9 KB/s	2.6 KB/s	2.6 KB/s
	Min	209.1 KB/s	0.1 KB/s	0.1 KB/s
	Max	622.9 KB/s	29.2 KB/s	26 KB/s
MQTT round-trip latency	# of samples	1440	1440	1440
	Mean	0.802 s	0.800 s	0.801 s
	Stdv.	0.787	0.8188	0.806

4 Conclusion

The proposed system architecture employs a network of distributed edge nodes that collect sensor readings from the environment as well as the solar photovoltaic panels and transmits them back to the main station over WiFi. In addition to maintaining a large-scale database, the main station hosts an application server that offers monitoring of readings in real time, an overview of historic data, geolocation-based visualization of connected solar farms, and big data analytics. The system is used to enable and support the study of the effects of environmental factors, on solar farm, such as dust accumulation and its effect on power generation efficiency. The system also enables stakeholders to monitor and control critical operations. This is made possible via Internet of Things communication, software, and hardware technologies which are inherently designed for large scale distributed ecosystems.

References

1. Burton, P.D., King, B.H.: Application and characterization of an artificial grime for photovoltaic soiling studies. IEEE J. Photovoltaics **4**, 299–303 (2014). https://doi.org/10.1109/JPHOTOV.2013.2270343
2. Zapata, J.W., Perez, M.A., Kouro, S., et al.: Design of a cleaning program for a pv plant based on analysis of energy losses. IEEE J. Photovoltaics **5**, 1748–1756 (2015). https://doi.org/10.1109/JPHOTOV.2015.2478069
3. Liu, H., Nobre, A.M., Yang, D., et al.: The impact of haze on performance ratio and short-circuit current of PV systems in Singapore. IEEE J. Photovoltaics **4**, 1585–1592 (2014). https://doi.org/10.1109/JPHOTOV.2014.2346429
4. Huang, P., Zhao, W., Li, A.: The preliminary investigation on the uncertainties associated with surface solar radiation estimation in Mountainous Areas. IEEE Geosci. Remote Sens. Lett. **14**, 1071–1075 (2017). https://doi.org/10.1109/LGRS.2017.2696973
5. Khoo, Y.S., Nobre, A., Malhotra, R., et al.: Optimal orientation and tilt angle for maximizing in-plane solar irradiation for PV applications in Singapore. IEEE J. Photovoltaics **4**, 647–653 (2014). https://doi.org/10.1109/JPHOTOV.2013.2292743
6. Rahman, M.M., Selvaraj, J., Rahim, N.A., Hasanuzzaman, M.: Global modern monitoring systems for PV based power generation: a review. Renew. Sustain. Energy Rev. (2017). https://doi.org/10.1016/j.rser.2017.10.111
7. Degener, S.: The internet of things: enabling intelligent solar assets. Renew. Energy Focus **17**, 136–137 (2016). https://doi.org/10.1016/j.ref.2016.06.004
8. Adhya, S., Saha, D., Das, A., et al.: An IoT based smart solar photovoltaic remote monitoring and control unit. In: 2016 2nd International Conference on Control, Instrumentation, Energy Communication (CIEC), pp. 432–436 (2016)
9. Jihua, Y., Wang, W.: Research and design of solar photovoltaic power generation monitoring system based on TinyOS. In: 2014 9th International Conference on Computer Science Education, pp. 1020–1023 (2014)
10. Liu, G., Qiu, H., Zhu, L., Chen, Y.: Architecture and experiment of remote monitoring and operation management for multiple scales of solar power plants. In: 2017 IEEE 2nd Advanced Information Technology, Electronic and Automation Control Conference (IAEAC), pp. 2489–2495 (2017)

11. Mashal, I., Alsaryrah, O., Chung, T.-Y., et al.: Choices for interaction with things on Internet and underlying issues. Ad Hoc Netw. **28**, 68–90 (2015). https://doi.org/10.1016/j.adhoc.2014.12.006
12. Yokotani, T., Sasaki, Y.: Comparison with HTTP and MQTT on required network resources for IoT. In: 2016 International Conference on Control, Electronics, Renewable Energy and Communications (ICCEREC), pp. 1–6 (2016)
13. Naik, N.: Choice of effective messaging protocols for IoT systems: MQTT, CoAP, AMQP and HTTP. In: 2017 IEEE International Systems Engineering Symposium (ISSE), pp. 1–7 (2017)
14. Yocto-Amp - Tiny isolated USB ammeter (AC/DC). http://www.yoctopuce.com/EN/products/usb-electrical-sensors/yocto-amp. Accessed 27 Mar 2017
15. nmon for Linux | Main / HomePage. http://nmon.sourceforge.net/pmwiki.php. Accessed 27 Mar 2017
16. Kansal, P., Bose, A.: Bandwidth and latency requirements for smart transmission grid applications. IEEE Trans. Smart Grid **3**, 1344–1352 (2012). https://doi.org/10.1109/TSG.2012.2197229

A Smart Meter Firmware Update Strategy Through Network Coding for AMI Network

Syed Qaisar Jalil[1(✉)], Stephan Chalup[1], and Mubashir Husain Rehmani[2]

[1] The University of Newcastle, Callaghan, Australia
syedqaisar.jalil@uon.edu.au
[2] Waterford Institute of Technology (WIT), Waterford, Ireland

Abstract. With the introduction of communication infrastructure into the traditional power grids, smart power grids are emerging to meet the future electricity demands. In smart grid, advanced metering infrastructure (AMI) is one of the main components that enables bi-directional communication between home area networks and utility providers. In an AMI network, one of the crucial operations is to update the firmware of the smart meters. In this paper, we propose a new forwarding strategy for the firmware updates in AMI network. Our simulation results show that the completion time of the smart meter firmware update process can be reduced significantly by using the proposed new strategy.

Keywords: Network coding · Firmware updates · Smart grid
Neighbourhood area networks · Advanced metering infrastructure

1 Introduction

In traditional power grids, electric power flows only in one direction, i.e. from the power generating stations to the consumers via large interconnected networks. Information is only monitored in the distribution networks that distribute the electric power to the individual consumers [1]. These power grids will not be able to support the future electricity demands due to the ageing infrastructure, growing energy demands, emerging renewable energy sources and security problems. Smart grid (SG) paradigm has been introduced to meet the future electricity demands. SG is envisioned to integrate the bi-directional communication, control technology, and sensing into the power system to achieve significant improvements in reliability, sustainability, stability and security of the electrical grid [2].

In SG, AMI is the architecture that enables two-way communication between home area networks and the utility provider [3]. AMI includes smart meters, communication system and a meter data management system. AMI plays a significant role in the working of SG by measuring, collecting and analysing energy usage patterns. To provide these functionalities, AMI must support a

A.-S. K. Pathan et al. (Eds.): SGIoT 2018, LNICST 256, pp. 68–77, 2019.
https://doi.org/10.1007/978-3-030-05928-6_7

variety of traffic generated from different sources (utility, data concentrators and smart meters) along with the constraints like limited bandwidth and time critical applications [4].

The smart meter is an advanced energy meter that provides functions like data collection, data storing, load control, display and billing [5]. A smart meter comprises the network interface card (NIC), processor and other electronic parts which can process the information and communicate it over the communication network. It has the ability to run TCP/IP suite as well as can use TCP or UDP. Moreover, the operating system of a smart meter can support a range of applications which enables it to perform tasks like measurement, database management and communication [6]. The software which runs on the smart meter to control, monitor and manipulate the data is known as firmware. Smart meter vendors develop the firmware and update it regularly to improve the functionality, fix the detected bugs, and add new functionality to their smart meters [7]. Moreover, firmware is also useful for utility companies when they update their applications for functionality improvement, bug fixing or due to the changes of legal requirements.

Firmware updates are required to have 98% reliability and in some cases, are required to have a latency of 2 mins [8]. Such reliability is needed because of the fact that if the firmware of the smart meters is compromised, then the real-time monitoring and other functionalities of the SG are compromised too. Also, if there is a bug in the smart meters which hinders the process of demand response management, then the utility provider would want to update the firmware of the smart meters as soon as possible, otherwise it can lead to the high economic loss. Moreover, there is a considerable security threat involved in the firmware update process. For instance, a terrorist organisation can launch the firmware update in the SG which cannot only give them access to shut off the electricity to the customers but also damage the power generating facilities and SG infrastructure [9]. Therefore, in the event of a malicious code attack, some fallback measure must be present such that the smart meter vendors or utility companies can revert all smart meters to the safe mode and this should be done remotely and quickly.

In an AMI network, one of the critical operations is to update the firmware of the smart meters. However, there are only few publications on updating the firmware of smart meters, and most of the work in the literature has focused on the security aspects. Authors in [10] proposed a network service management system and firmware update management system and they also introduced remote firmware update process in AMI networks. To avoid malicious firmware updates, authors in [11] proposed a secure firmware update method based on the pre-defined pattern of changes in the base frequency. In [12], authors have proposed an attribute-based multicast-over-broadcast protocol for firmware updates in AMI network. This protocol makes use of ciphertext-policy attribute-based signcryption to provide access control, confidentiality and message authentication. Authors extended their work in [7] by employing random linear network coding to overcome the issue of reduced reliability imposed by the use of signcryption.

In this paper, we propose the firmware update process under a new cooperation strategy among the smart meters namely: most served neighbour forwarding firmware update (MSNFFU) and most neighbour forwarding firmware update with network coding (MSNFFU-NC). In our strategies, we utilise neighbour information and random linear network coding to speed up the process of the firmware updates. We compare our strategies with four other cooperation strategies namely: blind forwarding firmware update (BFFU), blind forwarding firmware update with network coding (BFFU-NC), selective forwarding firmware update (SFFU) and selective forwarding firmware update with network coding (SFFU-NC).

The organisation of the paper is as follows. Section 2 provides the background information about the NAN, AMI and RLNC. Section 3 introduces system model and problem definition. In Sect. 4, we present the solution and implementation details along with different cooperation strategies. Simulation results are also presented and discussed in this section. Finally, we summarise our work and conclude the paper in Sect. 5.

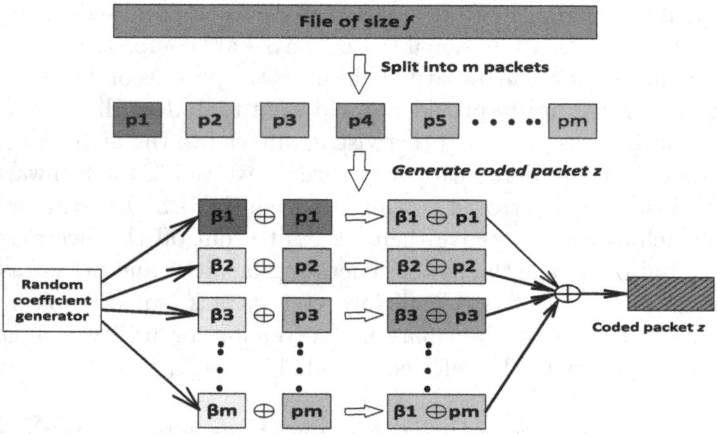

Fig. 1. In this figure, generation of the coded packet through RLNC is shown. $\beta 1, \beta 2, ..., \beta m$ are the random coefficients whereas, $p1$, $p2$, ..., pm are the packets (chunks) of the original file of size *f*. Addition operation ($\oplus$) is used to combine the random coefficients and chunks. Then, again addition is performed over the combined packets to generate the coded packet *z*.

2 Preliminaries

Neighborhood Area Networks and Advance Metering Infrastructure. Communication in SG can be broken down into following three main network types. Firstly, home area network (HAN) which is responsible for the communication of sensors and devices inside the home. Secondly, neighbourhood area network (NAN) which is responsible for connecting smart homes (smart meters) and concentrators. Finally, wide area network (WAN) which is responsible for the communication between concentrators and the utility control centres [1].

In NAN, smart meters are connected in a mesh topology along with a concentrator such that total connectivity is ensured. Smart meters generate data which is then collected by the concentrators and forwarded to the control centre using WAN. Moreover, pricing and control messages are delivered in the reverse direction by the concentrators. Since smart meters are nodes, we will use the term "smart meter" and "node" interchangeably. It is worth mentioning that NANs consists of thousands of nodes which are deployed in complex and large geographical areas. Therefore, NANs play an essential role in SG communication [13].

Random Linear Network Coding (RLNC). Random linear network coding is utilized in the broadcast based communication because it produces close-to-optimal throughput and does not require a centralized controller for encoding/decoding operations [14]. In RLNC, data is divided into generations by the data source for broadcasting. There are m number of packets in a generation denoted by p_k where $k = 1, 2, ..., m$. Each packet has a size of q bytes. To obtain an encoded packet, a random linear combination of all the packets are computed in a generation. The encoded packet for each generation can be written as

$$z = \sum_{k=1}^{m} \beta_k p_k \tag{1}$$

where $\boldsymbol{\beta}_k$ is encoding vector. The encoding process of RLNC is illustrated in Fig. 1. In order to decode a packet, an encoding vector is required, which is included in every packet. Upon receiving an encoded packet, the receiver checks if the received packet is useful or not by checking the linear dependency of the encoding vector with all other possessed encoded packets. If the linear dependency is found then the received packet is discarded. On the other hand, the receiver keeps the packet (also known as the innovative packet) in the buffer and tries to decode the packets stored in the buffer.

Each entry of the encoding vector $\boldsymbol{\beta}$ is chosen randomly from Galois field $GF(2^i)$ where i is a positive integer. It is important to note that the Galois field is a finite field which means that the number of elements in it is finite and all the operations defined in it are closed. Therefore, the resultant of any operation from this field on two elements will be in the same field.

3 System Model

We consider a scenario of NANs where n fixed smart meters connected in a mesh topology are deployed in a square of area a. Each node has a well defined transmission radius r. To ensure the total connectivity among nodes, we chose the values of a, n and r by following the inequality $n \geq \frac{10 \cdot a}{\pi \cdot r^2}$ presented in [15].

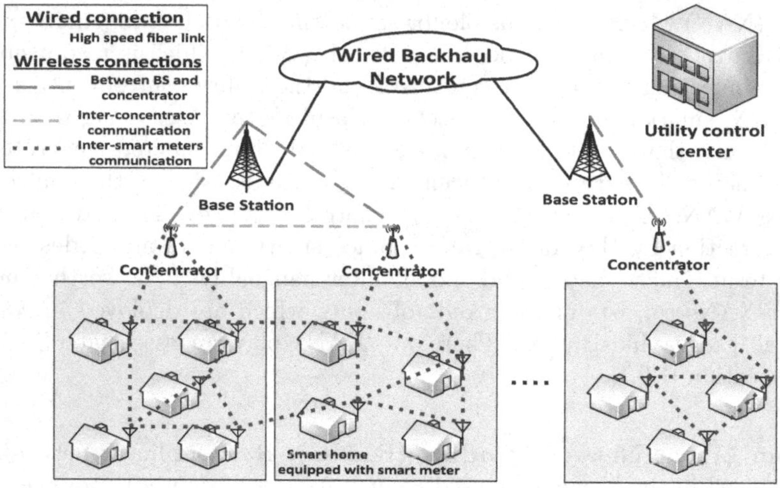

Fig. 2. Illustration of the smart grid communication architecture. Smart homes equipped with smart meters are connected in a mesh topology using wireless medium. Some of the smart homes are connected to concentrators that ensure the total connectivity of the network. Concentrators are connected to the base stations which in turn are connected to the utility control centre through WAN.

There is a number of c_t concentrators in the system which are connected to the control center through WAN. Here, it is important to mention that concentrator placement itself is a research problem [16] and this is beyond the scope of this paper. Therefore, we have only considered the case of concentrators at the extreme of the area a. The considered network model is illustrated in Fig. 2.

Concentrators have a firmware update patch of size f which is divided into $|m|$ chunks and needs to be disseminated in the system. γ is the available rate at which nodes can transmit file chunks over the wireless medium. The time required to download one single chunk and the entire firmware patch at rate b are defined as *one round* and *one unit of time*, respectively. Therefore, if there is a file of size f divided into |m| equivalent chunks then one round will be equal to $\frac{1}{|m|}$ unit of time.

We assume that the utility provider or smart meter vendors can determine the firmware of smart meters which needs to be updated. In the case of an update, the concentrator(s) will be notified and required to release the firmware update patch in the network such that the firmware is updated as soon as possible. A firmware update is a crucial operation because it might be happening in the case of a serious bug which, if delayed, can result in enormous economic loss. Therefore, the firmware update process should be performed in a time efficient manner.

4 AMI Firmware Updates Strategies

We consider six different AMI firmware updates strategies among nodes where three of these strategies make use of network coding. We adopted the first four strategies from the study [17] where authors have used the network coding for file sharing application in the wireless mesh network. In the first two strategies, we use the concept of flooding with and without network coding. Whereas, in the last four strategies, we assume that every node in the network has a neighbour information table, i.e. a list of available chunks at neighbours. Considering that smart meters have the capability to manage the database [6], and importance of the firmware updates, it is reasonable to assume such strategies where smart meters can maintain a table. However, building and maintaining such tables is beyond the scope of our paper. These strategies will ensure when and how network coding can be used in the process of smart meter firmware updates.

1. **Blind Forwarding Firmware Update (BFFU)** is a primitive cooperation strategy which is based on flooding. In this strategy, when a node receives a chunk, it tries to get access to the wireless medium. Upon getting access to the wireless medium, a node transmits the chunk to its neighbours without considering if any neighbour is interested in this chunk or not. Before performing a single transmission, a node may receive multiple chunks from the neighbours due to the shared wireless medium. Moreover, the order of reception of the chunks determines the transmission sequence of the chunks, i.e. first received chunks will be transmitted first.
2. **Blind Forwarding Firmware Update with Network Coding (BFFU-NC)** is same as the BFFU, but it uses network coding before transmission. In this strategy, upon receiving a new combination and getting access to the wireless medium, a node generates combination of all chunks (that are in the possession of this node) and forwards it to the neighbour nodes.
3. **Selective Forwarding Firmware Update (SFFU)** make use of the assumption that every node contains a table that has information about the neighbours, i.e. the list of chunks available at the neighbours. In this strategy, every node checks its table continually, and if it finds a chunk which is required by one of its neighbours, then this node transmits that particular chunk.
4. **Selective Forwarding Firmware Update with Network Coding (SFFU-NC)** is similar to the SFFU but it utilises network coding during transmission. Identical to the SFFU, every node checks its table continually, and upon finding a chunk of interest to its neighbour, this node generates the combination of all the information that it posseses and transmits it.
5. **Most Served Neighbour Forwarding Firmware Update (MSNFFU)** is similar to the SFFU, i.e. every node has a table which has the information of available chunks at its neighbours. In this strategy, a node is selected for transmission based on the number of neighbours it can satisfy, i.e. how many of its neighbours require a chunk that is available at this node. A priority queue of nodes, where the node that can serve most neighbours is first in

the queue, is created in each round. If there are many nodes with the same priority, then the first from the queue is selected.

6. **Most Served Neighbour Forwarding Firmware Update with Network Coding (MSNFFU)-NC** is similar to the MSNFFU, i.e. every node has a table which has the information of available chunks at its neighbours, but it utilises network coding during transmission. Similar to the MSNFFU, a priority queue is created in each round based on the number of neighbours a node can satisfy, but the transmission is different from MSNFFU. When a node is selected for transmission, it generates the combination of all the information that it posseses and transmits it. Pseudo code for MSNFFU-NC is presented in Algorithm 1.

4.1 Implementation Details

The proposed cooperation strategies were implemented in C++. We have taken the implementation code from [17] and modified it according to our scenario. Here, it is important to mention that the implementation considers a collision-free medium access control (MAC) protocol that gives the same probability to all the competing nodes to access the medium.

As stated earlier, the time-space is divided into rounds which enables us to analyse the distribution of the firmware patch among the nodes in the network. Transmission can only occur at the beginning of the round. The following four steps are performed in each round for transmission of chunks among the nodes.

In the first step, nodes which have chunks to send are identified and saved in the candidates list. Initially, only the concentrators have the patch; therefore, they are placed in the candidates list but later on, when the file chunks propagate in the network then other nodes will be added to this list. Assuming the collision-free MAC protocol, transmission can only be performed by some of the nodes in the candidate list. Therefore, we select the nodes that can perform transmission in the second step. We begin this step by randomly choosing a node from the candidates list and place it in a new list called the transmitters list. To ensure collision-free transmission, we look for the neighbours of the selected node and delete them from the candidates list. We also remove the neighbours of the neighbours of the selected node to avoid the hidden terminal situation.

It can be seen that the transmission selection criteria are fair and simple and gives the same chance, to all the nodes, to access the medium. The selection of the nodes from the candidates list is performed until it becomes empty. Then, in the third step, nodes from transmitter list perform transmission, i.e. transmit one chunk each. Finally, an update of the list of chunks at all nodes is performed in the fourth step. The above mentioned steps are performed continuously until the firmware patch is completely disseminated in the network.

4.2 Performance Evaluation

We conducted simulations for randomly created topologies of 100, 200, 300, 400 and 500 nodes. In every case, there was one concentrator that was placed at

Algorithm 1. MSNFFU-NC

```
while update patch is not disseminated in the network do
    for every node in network do
        check the neighbors table
        if node has chunk(s) required by neighbors then
            candidates_list ← node
        end if
    end for
    Based on the number of neighbours a node can serve, sort the candidates_list in
descending order
    while candidates_list is not empty do
        node_ ← select first node from candidates_list
        delete neighbors and neighbors of neighbors of selected node_
        transmitters_list ← node_
        delete selected node_ from candidates_list
    end while
    for every node in transmitter_list do
        generate random coefficient from Galois field
        create coded packet of all chunks
        perform transmission
        update nodes
    end for
end while
```

the extreme of area *a*. The reason for considering different numbers of nodes with one concentrator is to generalise our results for rural and urban areas, i.e. in urban areas, nodes are deployed more densely compared to rural areas. We divided the firmware update patch into 10 chunks. We considered completion time as a performance metric, i.e. the amount of time required to distribute the firmware patch in the system. We conducted simulations with 500 runs, and average values are shown in Fig. 3.

In Fig. 3, the completion time of different nodes with $|m| = 10$ for all strategies is plotted. We can see that BFFU has the worst completion time compared to other schemes and the reason is that it is based on flooding. In BFFU, a node will transmit the chunks even when none is interested in receiving the chunks; therefore, a lot of useless chunks are forwarded and this makes the process, of disseminating the actually required chunks, slow. When NC is incorporated in BFFU, its performance gets better. Now, the completion time of SFFU and SFFU-NC shows similar behaviour and the reason is that in SF only those chunks are transmitted by a node which is of interest to any of its neighbours. When NC is incorporated in SF, it results in an increased number of neighbours that are interested in each transmission. The completion time of MSNFFU is better than all above strategies because in this strategy nodes are selected for transmission based on the number of neighbours they can serve. Therefore, in each transmission the maximum number of nodes gets served; hence, the firmware update patch is disseminated quickly. Now, MSNFFU-NC has the most reduced

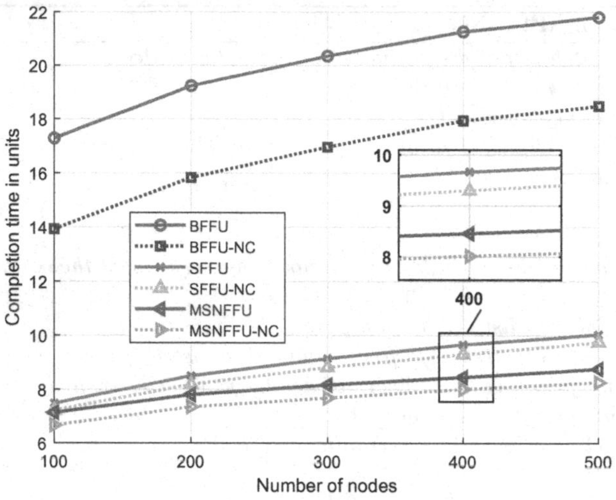

Fig. 3. Completion time vs number of nodes, where $|m| = 10, r = 5$

completion time compared to other strategies. It is even better than MSNFFU because, upon getting access to the medium, a node will generate the combination of all the information that it posseses and transmits. Whereas, in MSNFFU a node can only transmit one chunk at a time.

5 Conclusion

In this paper, we proposed a new forwarding strategy for the firmware updates in AMI networks. We compared our proposed approach with other different cooperation strategies. Through simulation experiments we demonstrated that our proposed MSNFFU-NC outperforms all other strategies and can reduce smart meter firmware update process time.

References

1. Khan, A.A., Rehmani, M.H., Reisslein, M.: Cognitive radio for smart grids: survey of architectures, spectrum sensing mechanisms, and networking protocols. IEEE Commun. Surv. Tutor. **18**(1), 860–898 (2016)
2. Wang, W., Xu, Y., Khanna, M.: A survey on the communication architectures in smart grid. Comput. Netw. **55**(15), 3604–3629 (2011)
3. Mohassel, R.R., Fung, A., Mohammadi, F., Raahemifar, K.: A survey on advanced metering infrastructure. Int. J. Electr. Power Energy Syst. **63**, 473–484 (2014)
4. Ramírez, D.F., Céspedes, S.: Routing in neighborhood area networks: a survey in the context of ami communications. J. Netw. Comput. Appl. **55**, 68–80 (2015)
5. Zheng, J., Gao, D.W., Lin, L.: Smart meters in smart grid: an overview. In: IEEE Green Technologies Conference (GreenTech), pp. 57–64 (2013)

6. Khalifa, T., Naik, K., Nayak, A.: A survey of communication protocols for automatic meter reading applications. IEEE Commun. Surv. Tutor. **13**(2), 168–182 (2011)
7. Tonyali, S., Akkaya, K., Saputro, N., Cheng, X.: An attribute network coding-based secure multicast protocol for firmware updates in smart grid AMI networks. In: 26th International Conference on Computer Communication and Networks (ICCCN), p. 19, July 2017
8. Khan, A.A., Rehmani, M.H., Reisslein, M.: Requirements, design challenges, and review of routing and MAC protocols for cr-based smart grid systems. IEEE Commun. Mag. **55**(5), 206–215 (2017)
9. Kropp, T.: System threats and vulnerabilities (power system protection). IEEE Power Energy Mag. **4**(2), 46–50 (2006)
10. Kim, Y., Oh, D., Ko, J., Kim, Y., Kang, S., Choi, S.-H.: A remote firmware upgrade method of NAN and HAN devices to support AMI's energy services. In: Lee, G., Howard, D., Ślęzak, D. (eds.) ICHIT 2011. CCIS, vol. 206, pp. 303–310. Springer, Heidelberg (2011). https://doi.org/10.1007/978-3-642-24106-2_40
11. Katzir, L., Schwartzman, I.: Secure firmware updates for smart grid devices. In: 2nd IEEE PES International Conference and Exhibition on Innovative Smart Grid Technologies, pp. 1–5 (2011)
12. Tonyali, S., Akkaya, K., Saputro, N.: An attribute-based reliable multicast-over-broadcast protocol for firmware updates in smart meter networks. In: IEEE Conference on Computer Communications Workshops (INFOCOM WKSHPS), pp. 97–102, May 2017
13. Meng, W., Ma, R., Chen, H.H.: Smart grid neighborhood area networks: a survey. IEEE Network **28**(1), 24–32 (2014)
14. Ho, T., Koetter, R., Medard, M., Karger, D.R., Effros, M.: The benefits of coding over routing in a randomized setting. In: IEEE International Symposium on Information Theory (2003)
15. Philips, T.K., Panwar, S.S., Tantawi, A.N.: Connectivity properties of a packet radio network model. IEEE Trans. Inf. Theory **35**(5), 1044–1047 (1989)
16. Aalamifar, F., Shirazi, G.N., Noori, M., Lampe, L.: Cost-efficient data aggregation point placement for advanced metering infrastructure. In: IEEE International Conference on Smart Grid Communications (SmartGridComm), pp. 344–349 (2014)
17. Hamra, A.A., Barakat, C., Turletti, T.: Network coding for wireless mesh networks: a case study. In: International Symposium on a World of Wireless, Mobile and Multimedia Networks (WoWMoM 2006), pp. 9-114 (2006)

Protected Bidding Against Compromised Information Injection in IoT-Based Smart Grid

Md Zakirul Alam Bhuiyan[1,2], Mdaliuz Zaman[1], Guojun Wang[2(✉)], Tian Wang[3], Md. Arafat Rahman[4], and Hai Tao[5]

[1] Department of Computer and Information Science, Fordham University, New York City, NY, USA
[2] School of Computer Science and Educational Software, Guangzhou University, Guangzhou, China
csgjwang@gmail.com
[3] Department of Computer Science and Technology, Huaqiao University, Xiamen, China
[4] Faculty of Computer Systems and Software Engineering, Universiti Malaysia Pahang, Pekan, Malaysia
[5] Department of Computer Science, Baoji University of Arts and Sciences, Baoji, Shaanxi, China

Abstract. The smart grid is regarded as one of the important application field of the Internet of Things (IoT) composed of embedded sensors, which sense and control the behavior of the energy world. IoT is attractive for features of grid catastrophe prevention and decrease of grid transmission line and reliable load fluctuation control. Automated Demand Response (ADR) in smart grids maintain demand-supply stability and in regulating customer side electric energy charges. An important goal of IoT-based demand-response using IoT is to enable a type of DR approach called automatic demand bidding (ADR-DB). However, compromised information board can be injected into during the DR process that influences the data privacy and security in the ADR-DB bidding process, while protecting privacy oriented consumer data is in the bidding process is must. In this work, we present a bidding approach that is secure and private for incentive-based ADR system. We use cryptography method instead of using any trusted third-party for the security and privacy. We show that proposed ADR bidding are computationally practical through simulations performed in three simulation environments.

Keywords: Internet of Things (IoT) · Smart grid · Demand response
Security attack · Privacy · Compromised information injection

1 Introduction

Considering Internet of Things (IoT) technologies in smart grid applications is an important method to expedite the informatization of power grid infrastructure. IoT is composed of embedded sensors and actuators, which senses and

A.-S. K. Pathan et al. (Eds.): SGIoT 2018, LNICST 256, pp. 78–84, 2019.
https://doi.org/10.1007/978-3-030-05928-6_8

controls the behaviors of the energy world. IoT is attractive for features of grid catastrophe prevention and decrease of grid transmission line and reliable load fluctuation control. Automated demand response (ADR) with IoT-based smart grids maintain facility for consumers to run a major role in optimizing energy consumption patterns, that is, decreasing or shifting their energy use during peak periods in response to time-based charges or other methods of economic inducements. It maintains demand-supply stability and in regulating customer side electric energy charges. Future IoT-based smart grid integrates demand response [4,9].

Demand bidding (DB) program is an important type of demand responses [8,11]. Southern California Edison (SCE) has recently approved DB program in practice. The consumer can pick a bidding charge as part of the consumer of energy usage discount. If the real quantity of energy reduction corresponds to given demand, the consumer gets rewarded. Alternatively, if the consumer cannot to save the energy usage according to the demand, no commercial punishment is incurred. An important goal of IoT-based smart grids is to enable a type of DR approach called automatic demand bidding (ADR-DB). Demand bidding is often considered to purchase sharing and allocation problem in energy usage market [4,11,14] (Fig. 1).

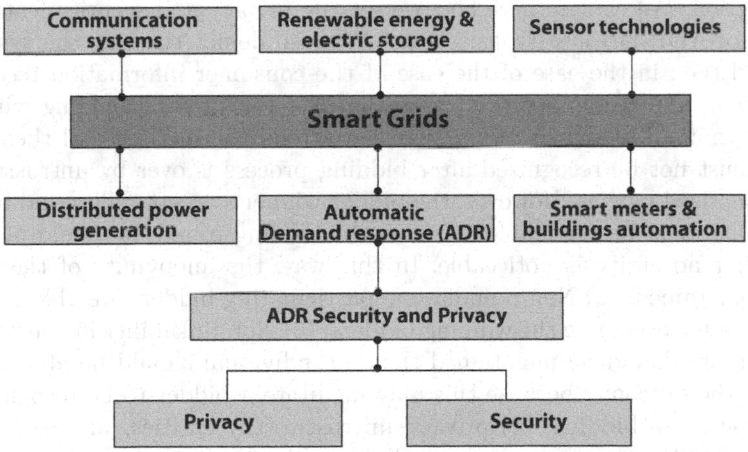

Fig. 1. Security and privacy concerns with ADR in smart grids.

2 Design of Protected Bidding in IoT-Based Smart Grid

An IoT-based smart grid is envisioned to be a fully automated system that can be to obtain decreased cost and better quality of service. These show potential benefits that are rigorously built on wide area measurement and control system, which is called WAMCS. This offers high-level detectability and manageability in energy grid functions. Subsequently, we consider the WAMCS as the system model in this work.

In smart grid, data is collected by the phasor measurement units (PMU). The data collected by PMUs provide the foundation for automatic, effective, and well-organized system management. But there can be cyber enemies or attackers who can come up with the purpose of interfering or basing the basic system functions and they can make an effort to introduce false information into the measurement data through intentionally deployed suspicious PMUs. Regarding the case of IoT-based network, collected data can be compromised at the time of data collection [6,10,12]. Successful false information board attack may compromise the auspicious functionalities described above. They can also ruin the total smart grid system functions. There are numerous threat models [2,3,5,7,13] for smart grid network. We consider that PMUs in the WAMCS, which might be attacked and colluded by the false information board that the attackers can make. For example, they can change and recode the programing interface and settings, or make disconnection in the interface and alter the privacy information board for data transmission and reception [1]. In the case of IoT-based smart grid network, if we consider only one false measurement information board, it might not be able to cause much influence on smart grid system functions. This reason is that the system can be enabled to correct minor errors and faults itself in the subsequent time.

We consider the security and privacy to protection unauthorized information injection. We explain here how we set the privacy and security features in the case of ADR-DB system as follows. We also depict the way the system is controlled (i.e., in the case of the ease of the consumer information recording, cancellation, and demand provision as the incentives to the bidding winners). (1) Anonymity–a bidder or bid winner can attend the bidding and their information must not be recognized after bidding process is over by untrustworthy or unauthorized parties. However, the bidder winner's acceptability and bidding information must be certifiable. Also, at the bidding round, it should be maintained that no entity is noticeable. In this way, the anonymity of the bidder can be maintained: (2) Non-repudiation–participating bidders are able to refuse their bids after becoming the winning bidders; (3) Non-linkability in a few rounds of bidding: it should be maintained that no individual should be able to have access to the outcome; because this may facilitate a bidder to be recognized in several rounds of bidding; (4) privacy–untrustworthy entities can be restricted who may find the chance to construct links to the bidding winner and to designated consumers; (5) Forward security: bidding is done with cryptography key, even if the existing bidding key is attacked, the system maintain security so that information board having the previous keys can be disclosed.

Regarding the given system model and threat models above, our objective is to design a protected and effective, and privacy-oriented ADR-DB bidding process for the IoT-based smart grid.

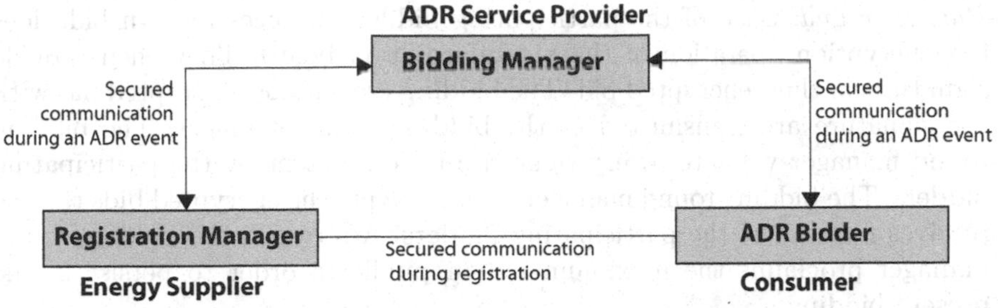

Fig. 2. System architecture for security and privacy in bidding process.

3 Architecture of Protected Bidding Process

We have three units in the architecture: (i) registration manager as the energy supplier, (ii) bidding round manager, and (iii) participating bidders. We maintain norms and definitions that are coherent to with open ADR specification. The registration manager uses privacy technique to distinguish the agreement and basic of the bidder's uniqueness in secret and bidder's cryptography-based registration key. Bidding round manager holds the bidding round process so as to make certificates for the bidding in every round. We can see in Fig. 2 that represents our system architecture.

4 Protocol Development

The protocol is comprised of the following phase:

- *Preparation phase.* At the beginning of a bidding session, a bidding round manager and a registration manager provide information board, where they can exhibit required data. These bidding information boards are usually read-only for individual and all other things. In addition, both of them produce factors and parameters to be used in the bidding protocol. It owns cryptography public- private key pair. For the security reason, it also has signing-verification key pair. Both jointly create an information board for the winning bidder.
- *Bidding key creation.* The registration manager transmits an authorized request to all the registered participating bidders. After the request is received and verified, all the participating bidders transmit the required information board, which is kept encrypted for producing the bidding round key to registration manager. The registration manager produces the bidding round keys and places the keys into the information board. Each participating bidder calculates its own bidding round key and saves it secretly.
- *Bidding round setup.* Using the parameters placed in registration manager's information board, the bidding round manager produces bidding credentials for each of participating bidders and places these credentials in their information board.

- *Bidding round.* Each of the participating bidder produces its own bid, does the encryption operation of the bid information board. They then provide signature on their encrypted bid. The bidding credentials, encrypted bid with the signature are transmitted to the bidding round manager. The bidding round manager validates every signature that was sent by the participating bidders. The bidding round manager then decrypts the encrypted bids that he receives from all of the participating bidders. Afterward, the bidding round manager proclaims the maximum bid in public in order to persist in the present bidding.
- *Bid validation.* Any participating bidder is permitted to examine the legality the bids across verifiable techniques.
- *Bidding winner declaration.* When the bidding round session is over, the bidding round manager declares the bidding winner's information. This information is usually placed on the bidding winner's information board. A participating bidder is able to verify and validate the winning bid.
- *Bidding incentive claim.* Once the bidding session is over, the bidding winner is allowed to demand the bidding incentive through a zero-knowledge proof placement to the registration manager.

As shown in Fig. 3, an UML illustration of bidding manager and other involvements in the bidding process shown in the protocol phases. Pre-processing phase is not given in the figure as it is considered to be pre-calculated. It shows that how compromised information can be injected during the bidding process.

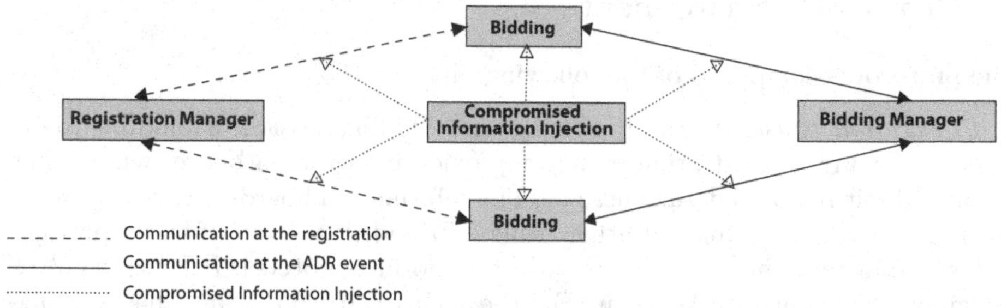

Fig. 3. Compromised information injection architecture.

5 Evaluation

We evaluate the protocol through simulations in Java in terms of primitive operations. These include modular multiplication (multiplying the two numbers and calculating the same modulus), modular exponentiation (a type of exponentiation performed over a modulus used for the public-key cryptography), modular multiplicative inverse and SHA-512 hash functions (producing an unique 512-bit signature). The bidding security key creation phase at the bidding registration manager is programmed regarding the primitives such as 5 modular exponentiations, 3 modular multiplications and two hashes (referring to the unique hash key when their hash code is equal). We carry out the simulation of each phase 50 times and gather the data. We then calculated the amount of time take in average. Figure 4 demonstrate the process of bidding cryptographic key creation. This usually consumes the highest amount of time between all the phases of the bidding registration manager, bidding round setup and bidding round session.

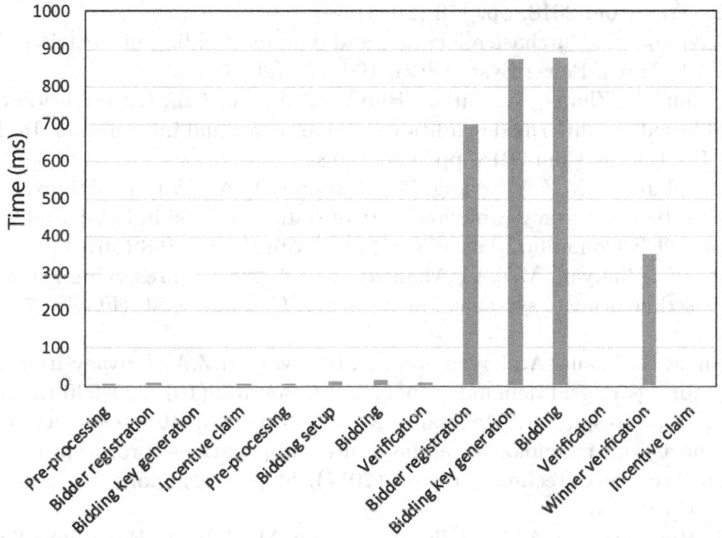

Fig. 4. Computation time needed for different phases.

6 Conclusion

Dealing with accurate information in the IoT-based smart grid infrastructure is significant regarding attacks situations and their severe consequences in the grid, hence, ensuring security and privacy is of great importance. Therefore, one key aim is to provide privacy and security in the ADR in order to prevent compromised information injection. Towards this, customers and demand response control should identify any unauthorized entities in the bidding process and reliability of the demand responses. In this paper, we have proposed a private and secure bidding protocol for incentive-based demand response system of IoT-based smart grids. The limitation of this paper is the performance evaluation of the security aspects of IoT based smart grid. Future work includes the detailed implementation of ADR bidding process in terms of security and privacy aspects.

References

1. Bhuiyan, M.Z.A., Wang, T., Hayajneh, T., Weiss, G.M.: Maintaining the balance between privacy and data integrity in Internet of Things. In: Proceedings of ACM ICMSS 2017, pp. 177–182 (2017)
2. Bhuiyan, M.Z.A., Wu, J.: Collusion attack detection in networked systems. In: Proceedings of IEEE DASC, pp. 1–8 (2016)
3. Liu, H., Xu, M., Wu, Y., Zheng, N., Chen, Y., Bhuiyan, M.Z.A.: Resilient bipartite consensus for multi-agent networks with antagonistic interaction. In: Proceedings of IEEE TrustCom 2018, pp. 1–8 (2018)
4. Liu, Y., Guan, X.: Purchase allocation and demand bidding in electric power markets. IEEE Trans. Power Syst. **18**(2), 106–112 (2003)
5. Lu, L., Zhu, X., Zhang, X., Liu, J., Bhuiyan, M.Z.A., Cui, G.: Intrusion detection method based on uniformed conditional dynamic mutual information. In: Proceedings of IEEE TrustCom 2018, pp. 1–7 (2018)
6. Luo, E., Bhuiyan, M.Z.A., Wang, G., Rahman, M.A., Wu, J., Atiquzzaman, M.: Privacyprotector: privacy-protected patient data collection in IoT-based healthcare systems. IEEE Commun. Mag. (COMMAG) **56**(2), 163–168 (2018)
7. Rahman, F., Bhuiyan, M.Z.A., Ahamed, S.I.: A privacy preserving framework for RFID based healthcare systems. Futur. Gener. Comput. Syst. (FGCS) **72**, 339–352 (2017)
8. Rahman, M.S., Basua, A., Kiyomotoa, S., Bhuiyan, M.Z.A.: Privacy-friendly secure bidding for smart grid demand-response. Inf. Sci. **379**(10), 229–240 (2017)
9. Saleem, Y., Crespi, N., Rehmani, M.H., Copeland, R.: Internet of Things-aided smart grid: technologies, architectures, applications, prototypes, and future research directions. Technical report (2017). https://arxiv.org/ftp/arxiv/papers/1704/1704.08977.pdf
10. Tao, H., Bhuiyan, M.Z.A., Abdalla, A., Hassan, M., Jain, J., Hayajneh, T.: Secured data collection with hardware-based ciphers for IoT-based healthcare. IEEE Internet Things J. (IEEE IoT-J), 1–10 (2018). https://doi.org/10.1109/JIOT.2018.2854714
11. Tarasak, P., Chai, C.C., Kwok, Y.S., Wah, S.: Demand bidding program and its application in hotel energy management. IEEE Trans. Smart Grid **5**(2), 821–829 (2014)
12. Wang, T., Bhuiyan, M.Z.A., Wang, G., Rahman, M.A., Wu, J., Cao, J.: Big data reduction for smart city's critical infrastructural health monitoring. IEEE Commun. Mag. (COMMAG) **56**(3), 128–133 (2018)
13. Wang, T., et al.: Fog-based storage technology to fight with cyber threat. Futur. Gener. Comput. Syst. (FGCS) **83**, 208–218 (2018)
14. Weng, Y., Negi, R., Faloutsos, C., Ilić, M.D.: Robust data-driven state estimation for smart grid. IEEE Trans. Power Syst. **8**(4), 1956–1967 (2017)

A Chain Based Signature Scheme for Uplink and Downlink Communications in AMI Networks

Samer Khasawneh(✉) and Michel Kadoch

Department of Electrical Engineering, École de Technologie Supérieure, University of Quebec, 1100 Rue Notre-Dame O, Montreal, Canada
samer.khasawneh.1@ens.etsmtl.ca,
michel.kadoch@etsmtl.ca

Abstract. Smart grid is an electric infrastructure that makes extensive use of communication and information technology making it a surface for numerous cyber-security threats. In this research, we propose an authentication scheme for downlink and uplink communications in the advanced metering infrastructure network. The proposal is based on chain based signature with some modifications to tackle its computation and storage overhead. Besides, the proposal integrates symmetric encryption with the signature scheme to ensure data privacy and confidentiality. Our analysis proves that the proposed scheme is resilient against numerous known attacks and is efficient in terms of computation cost and ciphertext size.

Keywords: Smart grid · AMI network · Security · Chain based signature

1 Introduction

In the past few years, strong pressure is generated to switch from the power generation that mostly based on fossil sources towards a modernistic smart system that highly incorporates renewable forms of energy [1]. The pressure was derived by the strong growth in electricity demand in addition to the emerging large quantities of distributed renewable energy sources.

The main attribute that characterizes the new power grid is integrating modern communication and information technology into the grid, making it smarter. The recent advances in communication and information technology can optimize the power grid performance by enabling us to generate, monitor, collect, analyze and react to data describing the grid's physical condition. However, it is no surprise that integrating communication and information technologies will result in a complex system-of-systems which requires a sophisticated architecture that is inherently Quality-of-Service (QoS) aware. The most widely accepted smart grid architecture viewpoint is the one that comprises seven domains: market, operations, service provides, bulk generation, transmission, distribution and customer [2], where the later four domains are the classic power system components.

A.-S. K. Pathan et al. (Eds.): SGIoT 2018, LNICST 256, pp. 85–99, 2019.

Advanced Metering Infrastructure (AMI) is the architecture that comprises smart meters at the customer's premises, data concentrators (gateways) and a supervisory node that acts as the AMI headend. Smart meters have multiple communication interfaces and are connected to various devices through a Home Area Network (HAN). It can collect information from the connected smart appliances to facilitate real-time billing. Smart meters can also issue commands to enforce peak demand management. Data concentrators preprocess the data received from the smart meters before having the data transmitted to AMI headend. Concentrators are stationed in physically secure locations such as substations. The supervisory headend node is located at the utility, within the company network. Basically, it acts on the smart meter's data and can issue several control commands such as pricing information updates, remote load control and demand response project's announcements. AMI systems enable near real-time pricing information and load exchange between the smart meters and utility business systems [3].

From the aforementioned description, it could be noted that AMI network realizes computerized two way communication between the metering network devices (in opposite to the conventional power grid that implements one way communication). Two-way communication is a smart grid feature that promotes implementing new functionalities such as Demand-Response, load shedding, peak shaving and self-healing [4]. In this case, QoS, reliability and real-time communication are critical performance factors.

1.1 Smart Grid Security

Smart grid is expected to optimize energy management, integrate renewable energy sources and introduce efficient billing schemes. Attaining such functionalities requires extensive use of information and communication technologies on a large-scale landscape. Accordingly, smart grid will be subject to significant cyber-security threats that will have negative impact on the grid services. Examples of such possible attacks are: Denial of Service (DoS), spoofing, replay, impersonation, data injection and privacy exposure (invasion) attacks. The degree of the damage caused by a cyber-attack depends mainly on the attacker skills and resources.

Achieving secure smart grid communication is crucial yet a challenging task for a number of reasons. First of all, the vast majority of the smart grid devices (especially the AMI devices) are equipped with limited storage, processing and communication capabilities. For this reason, some data encryption and authentication schemes could not be adapted for the smart grid. In addition, the lifetime of the power hardware is expected to be much longer than the information technology solutions. Therefore, a perfectly secure communication scheme is not expected to function during the whole lifetime of the power hardware. Another issue is the smart grid openness. The smart grid spans very large geographical areas and utilizes power devices from different manufactures which requires extremely high degree of interoperability between the grid systems and components. Finally, applying security measures may have counterproductive impact on the smart grid goals. For instant, a time critical packet may miss its deadline with the advanced authentication and integrity checks in place.

1.2 Our Contribution

The following are our contributions in this paper:

- We classified the AMI traffic into downlink and uplink traffic and associated the good transmission mode(s) for each one of them. This enables the network devices to efficiently generate and share the cryptographic keys without the need to maintain unnecessary keys.
- We have modified the basic chain based signature model to improve its computation and storage overhead. The modified signature scheme is used to propose an authentication model for downlink and uplink communications in AMI networks. A symmetric encryption is integrated with the signature scheme to ensure data confidentiality.
- Security analysis and performance evaluation are carried out to assess the feasibility of the proposed scheme. The results demonstrate that the proposed scheme is efficient in terms of computation cost and ciphertext size. In addition, it is capable to withstand various security attacks.

The rest of the paper is organized as follow. Section 2 reviews the related work. Section 3 demonstrates the models, design goals and background. The proposed encryption and signature scheme is illustrated in Sect. 4. The performance of the proposed scheme is presented in Sect. 4. Security analysis is presented in Sect. 5. Finally, the paper is concluded in Sect. 6.

2 Related Work

Nowadays, smart grid security is considered one of the most active research areas that attracted the researcher's attention. Despite the fact that the problem of security in the smart grid has not been fully identified, several researches have been proposed in the literature to address it. A zero-configuration identity-based signcryption for end-to-end communication in the advanced Metering Infrastructure (AMI) networks is proposed in [5]. The proposal has two phases of operation: registration phase and data transmission phase. In the registration phase, a device communicates with a Key Generation Server (KGS) to obtain a private key. The private key is used either to decrypt a received message or to sign a message before transmitting it. In the transmission phase, the sender calculates the receiver's public key using information derived from the receiver's identity and encrypts the message using the public key calculated. As the public keys are generated from information that is derived from the sender identity, the scheme achieves low computation overhead.

Anonymous Key Distribution (AKD) scheme for smart grid networks is proposed in [6]. The scheme is based on identity based elliptic curve cryptography to provide smart meter anonymity and mutual authentication. The scheme has several advantages such as: avoiding the need for third trusted party and achieving low computation and communication overhead compared to other schemes [7]. The proposal is resilient against data and impersonation based attacks.

Saxena et al. proposed a signature scheme for delivering authentic critical and non-critical commands in smart grid networks [8]. The proposed scheme is based on a set of cryptographic hashing functions to generate the message hash code. The code is splitted into several substrings with a predetermined length. The hashing functions are also used to generate the asymmetric keys (public/private) that will be used for signing the messages. Despite the fact that the scheme is secure against some authentications attacks, it has one major limitation. The authors assume that the signature is only constructed at the supervisory node; thereby alternative nodes such as smart meters don't sign their messages. Consequently, customer privacy could not be efficiently preserved.

An identity based signcryption technique for smart grid residential tree network is presented in [9]. The model employs bilinear pairing signcryption and destination concealing to achieve data integrity, authenticity and to preserve customer privacy. The proposed technique is designed to secure downlink communication between the control center and smart meters. The control center simultaneously encrypts and signs the messages before forwarding them to the smart meters. The authors show that the proposed technique is efficient in terms of computation cost and ciphertext length when compared to other schemes such as [10, 11]. However, the functionality of the proposed scheme is considered limited as the security measures are applied to messages generated by the control center. The uplink traffic generated by smart meters is not secured although it usually carries privacy-sensitive information. Further, the model supports unicast transmission mode only.

Mahmood et al. proposed a mutual authentication protocol for smart grid devices in [12]. The protocol utilizes elliptic curve cryptography and hashing functions to achieve data authenticity. The authentication protocol depends on the Elliptic Curve Discrete Logarithmic Problem (ECDLP) to attain prefect forward secrecy. Further, the scheme is constructed to withstand different attacks such as replay, impersonation and Man-in-the-middle attacks. The authors declare that the proposed authentication procedure is lightweighted in terms of computation complexity in addition to communication and memory overhead. The performance of the proposed scheme in one-to-many communication paradigms is suspected.

3 Models, Design Goals and Background

3.1 Network and Communication Model

In our scheme, we assume the AMI network that comprises three devices namely: smart meters (SMs), gateways (GWs) and Supervisory Control Center (SCC) as shown in Fig. 1. SMs are responsible for reporting energy consumption in addition to receiving billing information, thereby are equipped with limited computation and communication power. SCC has unlimited computation and communication power enabling it to manage the grid operation through performing critical tasks such as load shedding and demand response handling. Gateways have important rule in routing information in bidirectional paths from/to the SCC. The three devices can simultaneously and asynchronously perform signcryption operations at any time.

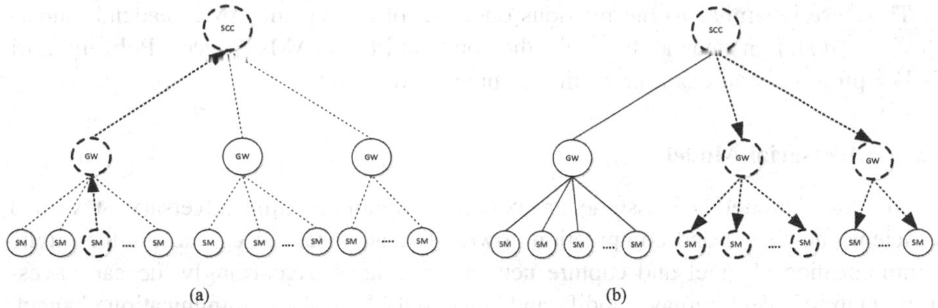

Fig. 1. The AMI communication models assumed in this paper. (a) Unicast uplink communication. (b) Multicast downlink communication

We have examined the communication paradigms that may exist between the three AMI devices and we have found that a communication in AMI network can fall in one of two categories:

a) *Uplink communication*

This communication is carried out when a lower layer device D_{LL} sends message to a higher layer device D_{HL}. For example, a smart meter transmitting to the corresponding gateway or a gateway that routes message to SSC. The transmission mode for such communication is unicast only.

– Unicast $(GW_i \rightarrow SSC, SM_i \rightarrow GW_i)$

Figure 1(a) shows an example of this case when a smart meter is reporting the customer's energy consumption to the corresponding gateway.

b) *Downlink communication*

In this case, a higher layer device D_{HL} sends message to a lower layer device D_{LL}. It could be the SCC transmitting to the corresponding gateway(s) or a gateway is routing messages to the corresponding smart meters(s). The transmission mode for such communication is unicast, multicast or broadcast.

– Unicast $(SSC \rightarrow GW_i, GW_i \rightarrow SM_i)$
  Remote load control is an example of this communication scheme. The supervisory node continuously monitors customer's consumption and can issue special command to enforce peak management.
– Multicast $(SSC \rightarrow GW_i, GW_i \rightarrow SM_i) i \in \{0, 1, \ldots l\} l < L$
  An example of downlink multicast AMI communication is shown in Fig. 1(b). Price updating and remote load control commands are triggered by the supervisory node and disseminated to certain Demand-Response projects in multicast transmission mode.
– Broadcast $(SSC \rightarrow GW_i, GW_i \rightarrow SM_i) i \in \{0, 1, \ldots L\}$

This case is similar to the previous one, except having the AMI headend (supervisory node) or gateway transmits the command to all AMI devices. Publishing of DR projects is an example of this communication style.

3.2 Adversarial Model

In our threat model, we assume an external polynomial time adversary $\mathcal{A}$ with a sufficient knowledge and computation power. The adversary $\mathcal{A}$ can access the public communication channel and capture network messages. Accordingly, he can eavesdrop, analyze, inject, replay, modify and delete data from the communication channel. Additionally $\mathcal{A}$ can compromise any smart meter (SM_i) or gateway (GW_i) and launch identity theft attacks later on. We assume the supervisory node (SCC) is securely suited within the utility premises and could not be compromised by the attacker.

3.3 Design Goals

Given the aforementioned adversarial model, our goal is to design an efficient encryption and authentication scheme for downlink and uplink communications in AMI networks. The model will be designed to take into consideration the requirements of each transmission mode for every communication direction. Practically, we aim to achieve the following three goals:

- *Authentication and Integrity.* The proposed scheme must guarantee that AMI messages injected or modified by the adversary $\mathcal{A}$ do not go undetected.
- *Confidentiality and privacy preservation.* Network messages (especially metering data) could be disclosed to authorize AMI participants only. The proposal should ensure that customer privacy never been infringed.
- *Efficiency.* The proposed encryption and authentication scheme should be lightweighted. It should be competent in terms of computation and communication cost compared to existing schemes.

3.4 Background

Chain based signature

t-time signature schemes could be constructed by combining a tuple of *t* independently generated private keys to form the private key, where the public key is constructed similarly. Each private/public key is used for a single signature generation/verification. Consequently, *t* signatures are generated using the tuple of private keys. The upper bound *t* should be determined in advance during the keys generation process. Such signature scheme has two main limitations. First, the number of signatures that could be constructed before re-invoking the key generation function is bounded. Second, the size of the cryptographic keys is large as each key consists of t individually generated keys. Chain-based signature scheme can achieve better performance in terms of key generation by allowing the signer to generate the cryptographic keys on the fly as needed.

Assume $\hat{C}$ = (***Gen***, ***Sign***, ***Vrfy***) a chain-based signature scheme, where ***Gen*** is the random key generation function that is used to generate the public and private keys on demand, ***Sign*** is the one way function that is used to construct the digital signature (σ) and ***Vrfy*** is the signature verification function. The operation of the chain-based scheme starts by having the signer generate a pair of cryptographic keys PK_0 and SK_0. In order to sign the first message m_0, the signer generates additional pair of keys (PK_1, SK_1), append the public key PK_1 to the message m_0 and signed the result using ***Sign*** and the private key SK_0 to obtain the signature $\sigma_0 \leftarrow Sign_{sk_0}(m_0||PK_1)$. PK_1 is generated and shared with the verifier in advance to enable verifying the message that will be signed next. Additionally, the signer has to store the state $\{m_0, PK_1, SK_1, \sigma_0\}$ to enable obtaining correct chaining between the signed messages. Subsequent messages are signed using the same procedure. For example, to sign the ith message m_i, ***Gen*** is invoked to generate the key pair (PK_{i+1}, SK_{i+1}), m_i and PK_{i+1} are signed using SK_i to obtain the signature $\sigma_i \leftarrow Sign_{sk_i}(m_i||PK_{i+1})$. The state $\{m_i, PK_{i+1}, SK_{i+1}, \sigma_i\}_{j=0}^{i-1}$ is added to the signer states. The signature that will be outputted includes σ_i, the next public key in the chain (PK_{i+1}) and the states $\{m_i, PK_{i+1}, SK_{i+1}, \hat{S}_i\}_{j=0}^{i-1}$ as well.

Verifying the signature σ_i of message m_i requires the verifier to validate (a) the lastly generated public key PK_{i+1} that is attached to m_i (b) the link between every consecutive public keys PK_j and PK_{j+1} in the signature chain. The verification function outputs 1 (as an indication of successful verification) if and only if ***Vrfy*** (PK_j, $\hat{S}$, $m_j||PK_{j+1}$) outputs 1 for all $j \in \{0, \ldots, i-1\}$. Accordingly, the verification process begins with the firstly generated public key PK_0 and goes with all public keys on the chain until PK_{i-1}.

Elliptic Curve Digital Signature Algorithm (ECDSA)

ECDSA is a public key algorithm that was accepted in 1999 as an ANSI standard as a substitute to the Digital Signature Algorithm (DSA). It is based on elliptic curve cryptography; which yields a security level compared to that of other public key schemes but with smaller key length. The strength of ECDSA comes from the need for solving the Elliptic Curve Discrete Logarithm Problem (ECDLP). ECDSA involves the use of three algorithms: key generation, signing construction, and signature verification. The key generation algorithm computes the private key (d) and the public key ($Q = dG$) to use in the verification and signature, respectively. In the proposed scheme, we implement the chain based signature using ECDSA.

4 The Proposed Scheme

In this section, we propose a crossbred encryption and signature scheme to confront confidentiality, integrity and authentication threats in AMI network. Symmetric encryption is employed to suit the requirement of low computation overhead.

In our scheme, the digital signature is constructed using a low complexity chain based algorithm. We assume a two-way AMI communication network where meters and SCC bidirectionally exchange data and control messages throughout the intermediate gateways. We address two communications flows namely: downlink and uplink. Downlink

Table 1. Notation guide

Notation	Description	Notation	Description
a, b, q, G, n, h	Elliptic curve parameters	$\boldsymbol{Sign}_{KS_i}$	Signature generation function
N_o	An adversary	$\boldsymbol{Vrfy}_{PK_i}$	Signature verification function
D_{LL}	Lower layer device	M_t	AMI message
D_{HL}	Higher layer device	$\overline{M}_t$	Encrypted AMI message
N_t	Initial nonce	ID_{LL}	ID of Lower Layer device
N_t	Nonce of session t	σ	Digital signature
$h_1(.), h_2(.)$	Hashing functions	l	Multicast domain size
k_{sh}	DH shared symmetric key	L	Broadcast domain size
k_U, k_M, k_B	Symmetric encryption keys for unicast, multicast, broadcast	$\|point\|$	Size of elliptic curve point including x and y coordinates
$KP_{UD}, KP_{MD}, KP_{BD}$	Public downlink unicast, multicast, broadcast keys for signature verification	$PGen(b)^1$	Asymmetric key generation function
$KS_{UD}, KS_{MD}, KS_{BD}$	Private downlink unicast, multicast, broadcast keys for signature generation	$SGen(b)^1$	Symmetric key generation function
PK_{UU}	Public uplink unicast signature verification key	$SYMM.ENC_k$	Symmetric encryption algorithm
SK_{UU}	Private uplink unicast, multicast, broadcast keys for signature verification	$SYMM.DEC_k$	Symmetric decryption algorithm

traffic is disseminated by SCC towards the smart meters and could have unicast, multicast or broadcast modes, whereas uplink traffic originated from the meters is unicast. The proposed scheme runs in two phases that are described in the following subsections.

4.1 Initialization Phase

The phase is demanded when a new smart meter or gateway joins the AMI network. The device initiates the initialization procedure with the corresponding gateway or SCC, respectively. In our scheme, the device that initiates the procedure is the *Lower Layer Device* D_{LL}, while the device that receives the initialization request is the *Higher Layer Device* D_{HL}. Consequently, D_{LL} is a smart meter or gateway and D_{HL} is a gateway or the SCC. This phase is required to enable D_{LL} and D_{HL} to securely set up the cryptographic parameters (keys and hash functions) over the inherently insecure AMI channels. D_{HL} assembles the elliptic curve parameters and shares them with D_{LL} to enabling generating the shared secret key K_{sh} based on Elliptic Curve Diffie Hellman (ECDH) protocol.

Downlink traffic is generated by D_{HL} and is transmitted to one or more D_{LL} devices in unicast, multicast and broadcast mode. Therefore, three secret keys $\{k_U, k_M, k_B\}$ are shared with D_{LL} to enable decrypting D_{HL} message's. Similarly, three public keys $\{KP_{UD}, KP_{MD}, KP_{BD}\}$ are securely shared with D_{LL} to enable verifying signatures constructed using the private keys $\{KS_{UD}, KS_{MD}, KS_{BD}\}$. On the other hand, uplink traffic is generated by D_{LL} and is transmitted to a single D_{HL} in unicast mode only. Consequently, one public key PK_{UU} need to be shared with D_{HL} to enable it verifies the signatures constructed using D_{LL} private key SK_{UU}. Additionally, D_{HL} randomly chooses an initial nonce value N_0 and shares it with D_{LL}. As we will demonstrate later in Sect. 6, using nonce can detect replay attack.

4.2 Encryption and Authentication Phase

In our model, two or more AMI participants can communicate securely by exchanging encrypted and signed messages. Symmetric cryptography is used to encrypt and decrypt the message content, while chain based signature is used to construct and verify the message signature (Fig. 2 and Table 1).

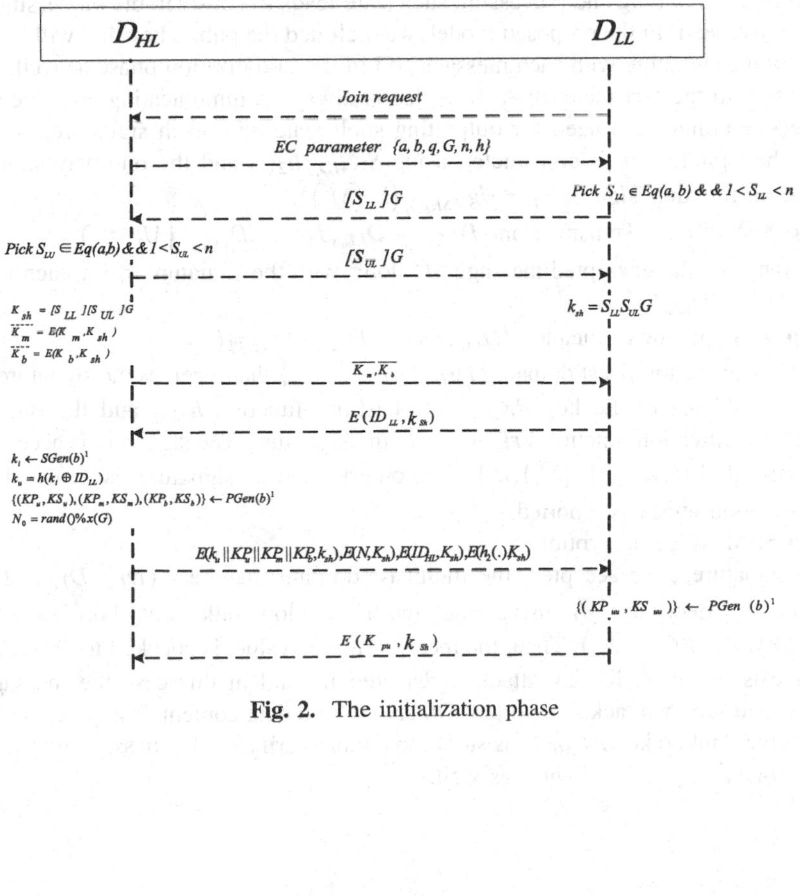

Fig. 2. The initialization phase

Now, suppose the multicast domain $\{D_{HL_1} \rightarrow D_{LL_i}, D_{LL_j} \ldots D_{LL_n}\}$ to enable gateway GW_1 delivering a remote load control message securely to the set of connect smart meters $\{SM_i, SM_j, \ldots\ldots SM_n\}$. The communication shall proceed as follows:

Step 1: Message construction Encryption $(D_{HL_1} : \{\overline{M}_t\})$
In the proposed model, the message to be encrypted has three components: the data content D, the nonce value $N_t = N_{t-1} + 1$ and a public key PK (multicast public key $PK_{MD_{t+1}}$ in this case). The nonce value is used to keep the parties in sync to ensure withstanding replay attack. Therefore, the transmitted nonce value is, N_{t-1} where $SYMM.ENC_{k_{MD}}(D||N_t||PK_{MD_{t+1}})$ is the nonce used in the previous session. In order to implement the chain based signature scheme, the public key that will be used by the receiver to verify the next signature must be sent a priori. Therefore, Asymmetric key generation function $PGEN$ is used to generate a pair of keys (PK_{t+1}, SK_{t+1}). The public key $PK_{MD_{t+1}}$ is attached to t^{th} message. The encrypted message $\overline{M}_t$ is $D_{LL_i}, D_{LL_j} \ldots D_{LL_n}: \{D, N_t, PK_{MD_{t+1}}\}$.

Step 2: Signature construction $(D_{HL_1} : \{\sigma_t\})$
As discussed in Sect. 3.4, the chain based signature outputs the state $\{m_i, PK_{i+1}, SK_{i+1}, \sigma_i\}_{j=0}^{i-1}$ with the signature σ_i to enable the receiver verifying the signature. Maintaining and processing such state leads to considerable processing and storage overhead. In the proposed model, we included the public key that will be used to verify the signature with each message and in the initialization phase as well. This, in addition to the fact the each AMI device is always communicating with the same device(s) eliminate the need for outputting such state with each signature. Accordingly, the signature σ_t is constructed using $SK_{MD_t}, h_2(.)$ and the one way signature generation function ***Sign*** as $\sigma_t = \boldsymbol{sign}_{SK_{MD_t}}(h_2(\overline{M}_t))$.

Step 3: Multicast Transmission $(D_{HL_1} \rightarrow D_{LL_i}, D_{LL_j} \ldots D_{LL_n} : \{M_t, \sigma_t\})$
D_{HL_1} transmits the encrypted message $\overline{M}_t$ along with the signature σ_t for each $D_{LL} \in \{D_{LL_i}, D_{LL_j} \ldots D_{LL_n}\}$

Step 4: Signature verification $(D_{LL_i}, D_{LL_j} \ldots D_{LL_n} : \boldsymbol{Vrfy}_{Pk}(.))$
Every D_{LL} in the multicast domain $\{D_{LL_i}, D_{LL_j} \ldots D_{LL_n}\}$ that receives the signature will use the multicast public key PK_{MD_t}, the hashing function $h_2(.)$ and the one way signature verification function ***Vrfy*** to verify the signature. The signature is accepted if and only if $\boldsymbol{Vrfy}_{PK_{MD_t}}(h_2(\overline{M}_t), \sigma_t) = 1$, otherwise the signature is rejected and impersonation attack is reported.

Step 5: Message decryption
If the signature σ_t is accepted, the multicast domain members $\{D_{LL_i}, D_{LL_j} \ldots D_{LL_n}\}$ individually decrypts $\overline{M}_t$ using the multicast downlink key k_{MD} to obtain $M_t = SYMM.DEC_{k_{MD}}(\overline{M}_t)$. Then, the received nonce value is checked to detect if the message is replayed. Replay attack is detected if and in this case the message is ignored and replay attack is reported. Otherwise, the data content D is processed and the received public key $PK_{MD_{t+1}}$ is stored to enable verifying the message that will be received next. is updated with as well.

Performance Evaluation

The efficiency of the proposed encryption and signature scheme can be evaluated in terms of the computation cost and ciphertext length. In this section, we present the performance of the proposed scheme and compare it with the signcryption model presented in [9].

4.3 Computation Cost

According to our scheme, the computation cost is the time overhead required to encrypt-sign the plaintext or verify-decrypt the ciphertext message. We implemented the chain based signature scheme using ECDSA where the elliptic curve point multiplication represents the most computation intensive operation. Symmetric cryptography, on the other hand, is very fast compared to public key cryptography. Therefore, the computation cost of our scheme is determined mainly by the time required to construct (sign) or verify a signature using the proposed chain based scheme, where point multiplication dominates ECDSA time.

Table 2 demonstrates a comparison between the computation cost required by our scheme and the signcryption scheme presented in [9]. The time required to generate the ciphertext in our mode is $T_{symm} + T_{mul}$ compared to $4 \times T_{mul} + T_{pair}$ for the signcryption scheme. Moreover, the time needed to recover the plaintext in our scheme is $2 \times T_{mul} + T_{symm}$ compared to $T_{mul} + 4 \times T_{pair}$ for the signcryption scheme.

Table 2. Computation cost: the proposed model vs. the signcryption scheme [9]

Scheme	Symmetric cryptography		EC point multiplication (T_{mul})		Pairing computation (T_{pair})	
	Our model	Model in [9]	Our model	Model in [9]	Our model	Model in [9]
Cipher-text generation	T_{symm}	–	1	4	–	1
Plaint-text recovering	T_{symm}	–	2	1	–	4

In order to show the numerical computation cost, we have done a computer simulation for two AMI networks, one implements our scheme and the another implements the signcryption scheme proposed in [9]. The simulation was executed on an Intel Pentium IV 3.1-GHz machine with 8 GB RAM. We have chosen AES-128 as the symmetric cryptography algorithm and SPEC112r1 standard [13] for elliptic curve encryption. The computation overhead of the two schemes is shown in Fig. 3. The total number of concurrent signatures creation or verification is determined by the number of smart meters in the AMI network. It is obvious that our scheme achieves lower computation cost compared to the signcryption scheme.

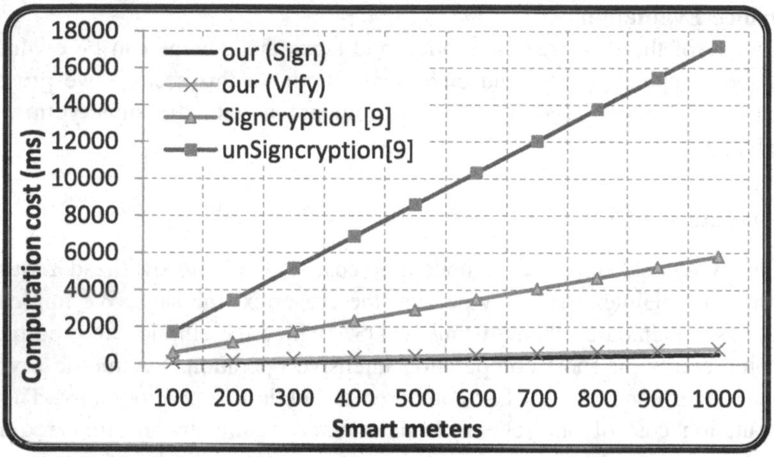

Fig. 3. Computation cost of the proposed scheme and the model in [9]

4.4 Ciphertext Size

Ciphertext ($\hat{C}$) size is the size of: the encrypted data, signature and any additional cryptographic parameters attached to enable recovering the plaintext. In the proposed scheme, the ciphertext $\hat{C} = (\overline{M}, \sigma)$, where $\overline{M}$ is the encrypted data and σ is the ECDSA signature.

AES encryption does not enlarge data size; therefore M and $\overline{M}$ both have the same size. The signature σ has two components (as per ECDSA details); hence the signature size is twice the length of the elliptic curve. Therefore, the ciphertext size is $|M| + |point|$. On the other hand, the ciphertext produced by the signcryption scheme presented in [9] is $\hat{C} = (C, C_{enc}, C_{sign})$. C and C_{sign} are each twice the size of the

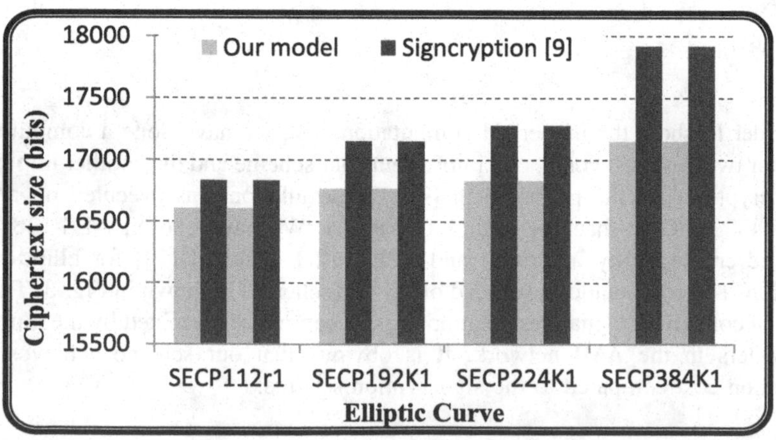

Fig. 4. Ciphertext size for different elliptic curves

elliptic curve as they are points on the curve. The scheme does not expand encrypted data too, therefore the size of the plaintext and C_{enc} are the same. The total length of the ciphertext under signcryption scheme will be $|M| + 2|point|$. Assuming a plaintext size of 16 KB, Fig. 4 illustrates the length of the resulting ciphertext under the proposed scheme and the one in [9] when using different elliptic curve standards.

5 Security Analysis

The proposed scheme provides encryption and authentication for downlink and uplink communication in AMI network. This section demonstrates the security analysis of the proposed scheme under the adversarial model presented in Sect. 3.2 by examining its resiliency against known attacks.

5.1 Passive Attacks

In order to guarantee data confidentiality, customer and supervisory node packets are never sent in clear, symmetric encryption algorithm *SYMM.ENC* (such as AES) is used to cipher those packets. Supervisory node (SCC) commands are encrypted using k_{UD}, k_{MD} *or* k_{BD} depending on the transmission mode, while customer metering data is encrypted using k_{uu}. Adversary $\mathcal{A}$ who intercepts AMI communication channels will not be able to collect any useful information concerning customer behavior or usage pattern. He will not be able to identify the remote load commands issued by SCC, as well.

5.2 Impersonation Attack

Adversary $\mathcal{A}$ can impersonate any D_{LL} or D_{UL} if he manage to forge their signatures. Under the proposed chain based signature scheme, the public keys $\{PK_{UD}, PK_{MD}, PK_{BD}, PK_{UU}\}$ are used once and they are sent encrypted a priori. Thereby, it will be impossible for the adversary $\mathcal{A}$ to gather and cryptanalyze combinations of legitimate public keys/signatures for the purpose of forging valid signatures. Hence, the proposed scheme withstands impersonation attack.

5.3 Replay Attack

The adversary $N_t \leq N_{t-1}$ can capture and store valid network messages for the purpose of maliciously replaying them later. Such attack is easily detected in our scheme by using nonce. At any time, the received nonce should be greater than its predecessor; therefore replay attack is detected when $N_t \leq N_{t-1}$. It should be noted that the attacker can't predict the current nonce value as the initial nonce is generated randomly and is sent encrypted.

5.4 Message Modification Attack

ECDSA is a secure public key algorithm because it is computationally infeasible to modify the message $\overline{M}_t$ and its signature σ_t to construct a new message with valid signature. Therefore, $\boldsymbol{Vrfy}_{PK}\left(h_2\left(\overline{M}_t\right), \sigma_t\right)$ function will output zero if the message or the signature (or both) are altered in transit. Hence, the attached digital signature can serve as a guard against message alteration and the proposed scheme withstand against message modification attack.

6 Conclusion

In this paper, we have proposed a chain based signature scheme to provide authentic two-way communication in AMI network. The proposed scheme employs symmetric cryptography as well, in order to maintain data confidentiality. For optimal implementation of the proposed scheme, we have classified the AMI traffic into downlink and uplink, and we examined the transmission mode(s) required by each class. We have shown that the proposed scheme can resist various known attacks and is efficient in terms of the computation overhead and the ciphertext length.

References

1. Abdulrahman, Y., Saifur, R.: Smart grid networks: promises and challenges. JCM **7**(6), 409–417 (2012)
2. Gungor, V.C., et al.: A survey on smart grid potential applications and communication requirements. IEEE Trans. Ind. Inform. **9**(1), 28–43 (2013)
3. NIST framework and roadmap for smart grid interoperability standards release 1.0 (2010)
4. Massoud, A.: A smart self-healing grid: in pursuit of a more reliable and resilient system [in my view]. IEEE Power Energy Mag. **12**(1), 110–112 (2014)
5. Hayden, K.-H. S., Sammy, H.M.K., Edmund, Y.L., King-Shan, L.: Zero-configuration identity-based signcryption scheme for smart grid. In: IEEE International Conference on Smart Grid Communications, October 2010
6. Debiao, H., Huaqun, W., Muhammad, K.K., Lina, W.: Lightweight anonymous key distribution scheme for smart grid using elliptic curve cryptography. IET Commun. **10**(14), 1795–1802 (2016)
7. Jia-Lun, T., Lo, N.-W.: Secure anonymous key distribution scheme for smart grid. IEEE Trans. SmartGrid **7**, 906–914 (2015)
8. Saxena, N., Grijalva, S.: Efficient signature scheme for delivering authentic control commands and alert messages in the smart grid. IEEE Trans. Smart Grid **9**, 4323–4334 (2017)
9. Alharbi, K., Lin, X.: Efficient and privacy-preserving smart grid downlink communication using identity based signcryption. In: 2016 IEEE Global Communications Conference, Washington, DC, pp. 1–6 (2016)
10. Libert, B., Quisquater, J.J.: New identity based signcryption schemes from pairings. In: IEEE Information Theory Workshop, Paris, France (2003)
11. Lal, S., Kushwah, P.: ID based generalized signcryption, Cryptology ePrint Archive http://eprint.iacr.org/2008/84 (2008)

12. Mahmood, K., Chaudhry, S.A., Naqvi, H., Kumari, S., Li, X., Sangaiah, A.K.: An elliptic curve cryptography based lightweight authentication scheme for smart grid communication. Future Gener. Comput. Syst. **81**, 557–565 (2018). https://doi.org/10.1016/j.future.2017.05.002
13. SEC 2: Recommended Elliptic Curve Domain Parameters, Certicom Research, 20 September 2000

Robustness Situations in Cases of Node Failure and Packet Collision Enabled by TCNet: Trellis Coded Network - A New Algorithm and Routing Protocol

Diogo F. Lima Filho[1(✉)] and José R. Amazonas[2]

[1] Universidade Paulista - UNIP, Rua Dr Bacelar, 1212, Vila Clementino, São Paulo, Brazil
dioferlima.usp@gmail.com

[2] Escola Politécnica, da Universidade de São Paulo, Av. Prof. Luciano Gualberto - Tr 3, 158, São Paulo, Brazil
jra@lcs.poli.usp.br

Abstract. This research exploits the new concept of route discovery using TCNet - Trellis Coded Networks an algorithm and routing protocol based on convolutional codes to be used in WSNs an important infrastructure of the Internet of Things (IoT) architecture. This work shows the robustness of the TCNet algorithm in making decisions in cases of nodes failure and packages collisions, taking advantage of the regeneration capacity of the trellis. This proposal innovates in making decisions on the node itself, without the need of signaling messages such as “Route Request”, “Route Reply” or the RTS and CTS. TCNet uses low complexity Finite State Machine (FSM) network nodes (“XOR” gates and shift registers), eliminating the use of any routing tables by means of Trellis decoding, where the sequence of states of the FSM, corresponds to a network route, and can be chosen based on different optimization criteria.

Keywords: Wireless sensor networks · Finite state machine · Nodes failure
Packages collisions · Trellis decoder · Trellis regeneration

1 Introduction

The constant searches to obtain protocols that support the WSNs networks are challenging due to the dynamic characteristics of these networks. Attempts to adapt the routing protocols of infrastructure networks to *ad hoc* networks are often inconsistent to identify issues such as: frequent changes in topologies, poor link quality, restricted bandwidth and power limitation.

The WSNs configure an *ad hoc* network scenario [1], where the nodes are the routers themselves due to the lack of network structure. In addition, the difficulty of links in covering large areas, suggests a distributed management of resources with intelligent protocols. *Ad hoc* devices can also be subjected to adversities that may render them inoperative. For these reasons, it is necessary that *ad hoc* networks must be

A.-S. K. Pathan et al. (Eds.): SGIoT 2018, LNICST 256, pp. 100–110, 2019.
https://doi.org/10.1007/978-3-030-05928-6_10

robust to failures so that important parameters such as latency, packet loss and energy consumption are not drastically affected.

This work proposes a new routing protocol based on convolutional codes addressed to *ad hoc* networks used to implement WSNs. It has been evaluated by means of efficiency analysis compared to the currently used traditional AODV [2] protocol that depends on the construction of routing tables, similar to RPL [3], both differing from TCNet that proposes a novel and different paradigm. This evaluation takes into account: latency and robustness in the presence of failures. To meet these characteristics, the protocol proposed in this research offers the following advantages that are compatible with the limited resources of WSNs:

- Elimination of routing tables;
- Reduced latency by eliminating the route request (RREQ) and route reply (RReply) signaling packets employed in protocols that use routing tables;
- Implicit self-recovery mechanism in case of failure.

1.1 Related Work

Over the past 15 years, routing in IP networks has been a topic of great interest and has led to the emergence of several routing protocols. The main function of the routing protocol is to determine the "best" path to reach a destination according to various metrics and objective functions.

Routing tables are populated in routers and indicate the best next hop for each reachable destination. Several routing protocols have been developed for intra-domain (e.g., AODV [2], RIP [4], IS-IS [5], OSPF [6], OLSR [7]) and inter-domain routing (e.g., BGP [8]).

Quality of Service (QoS) [9] is the network's ability to meet certain performance criteria such as network delay, jitter or packet drop probability and to perform a number of tasks in the network as packets are forwarded from the source to the destination.

The world of WSNs is no exception: The use of an open standard such as IP is crucial and is necessary to build a scalable architecture for the Future Internet and other IP networks. The Internet Engineering Task Force (IETF) represented by the Routing Over Low-Power and Lossy Networks (ROLL) Working Group [10] discussed a series of existing protocols, and to that end, defined the following set of requirements for WSN's network: routing metrics; scalability; network stability; degree of constraints and application aware routing as extremely challenging because of the high degree of network constraints.

1.2 Contributions and Proposal of the Paper

This work exploits the new concept of a "Trellis Coded Network" (TCNet) introduced by the authors in [11] for discovering the route to be followed by datagrams arriving at each of the network's nodes. The TCNet model explores the forward mechanism of routing protocols in analogy to Forward Error Correction (FEC) codes and its association with the states of a convolutional code. A trajectory in the convolutional code trellis representation corresponds to a path in the WSN and can be discovered by means of a Viterbi-based algorithm [12] proposed in 1967 for decoding convolutional codes based on the trellis diagram. TCNet implementation is on the level of proof-of-concept, and it can be easily adapted to work with IoT OSs like ContikiOS, TinyOS, FreeRTOS and others emerging OSs for the IoT [10].

This paper adds contributions to the proposal introduced in the previous work [11], where it will be shown the robustness of the process in case of nodes failures, and proposing solutions in cases of hidden and exposed nodes in WSNs. Briefly, such problems may be described as follows [13]:

- The hidden node problem refers to the collision of packets at a receiving node due to the simultaneous transmission of those nodes that are not within the direct transmission range of the sender, but are within the transmission range of the receiver, so both nodes transmit packets at the same time without knowing about the transmission of each other.
- The exposed node problem refers to the inability of the node that is blocked due to transmission by a nearby transmitting node to transmit to another node.

2 TCNet Algorithm Implementation Scenario

For a better understanding of the TCNet decoding mechanism, consider the example shown in the previous work [11]. The sink node initializes the frame loading the WSN header field with the information generated by the MM generator *($out_n(t)$ = (c1, c2))* and transfers the input sequence *({kn})* to the TCNet label field. Initially all nodes in the sink's node coverage area receive the request from it, Fig. 1a. Figure 1b shows the decoding trellis in which we realize that each node can only receive information from two other nodes. For example: node *(10)* receives information from node *(00)* when node *(00)* generates the code *(c1, c2)* = *(11)* and receives information from node *(01)* when node *(01)* generates the code *(c1, c2)* = *(00)*.

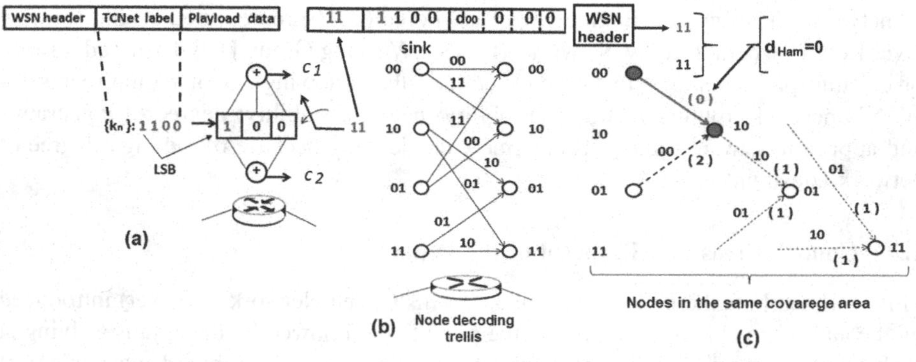

Fig. 1. (a) Initialization of the TCNet frame by the sink node: the input sequence *{kn}* is loaded on the TCNet label field and the output sequence $out_n(t)$ = *(c1, c2)* is loaded on the WSN header field; (b) Decoding trellis; (c) Nodes in the sink's coverage area receive the query.

Figure 1c shows the operations performed by each node when they receive the frame sent by the sink. For instance, node (10) evaluates d_{Ham} between the code received in the WSN header and the codes of the trellis branches, obtaining:

- from node (00) $\Rightarrow d_{Ham} = 0$
- from node (01) $\Rightarrow d_{Ham} = 2$.

The value $d_{Ham} = 0$ indicates that the received frame is for node (10) and it has come from the sink. Node (10) loads its information (value of the sensed variable) in the payload. Using the *{kn}* sequence received in the TCNet label, it determines that the next code *(c1, c2)* is (01) and updates the WSN header with that value.

For every other node that receives the frame from the sink, the procedure is performed, but none of them produce a value of $d_{Ham} = 0$. Therefore, these other nodes will not transmit and will wait to receive the next frame. This is a simple example to prove the validity of the concept proposed in this work.

3 TCNet Approach to Solve Node Failure and Package Collisions

Before introducing the TCNet approach to solve node failure and package collisions, this section starts by introducing the capability of trellis regeneration.

3.1 Network Recovery Capability Using Trellis Regeneration

The ability of TCNet to establish routes on a trellis is associated with the complexity of the Mealy machine (MM). The initial scenarios presented in this work use MM configuration with rate k/n = 1/2 and *hard decision* based on *Hamming distance* (d_{Ham}) [12] for the purpose of hardware simplifications, with implications in the reduction of the branches that leave the nodes, limiting the ability of decision of the trellis, as will be shown later.

An alternative to extend the options of connections between the nodes of a network is to use smoothing of the *Hamming distance*, through the concept of *soft decision* decoding, where the soft decision metric uses the concept of *free distance*$\left(d_{free}\right)$ [12]. This is possible by changing the inputs and outputs configurations of the MMs combined with changes in the quantities of symbols $\{v\}$ in the input sequence $k_n(t)$ (which indicates the route on the trellis), also corresponding to the quantities of connections leaving a node (e.g. $2^v = 2$ output, used with d_{Ham} in cases of *hard decision*). In cases of *soft decision* the node configurations are extended to $2^v = 4$ and $2^v = 8$ output or settings with more outputs, resulting in more branch options leaving the node, as the example in Fig. 2.

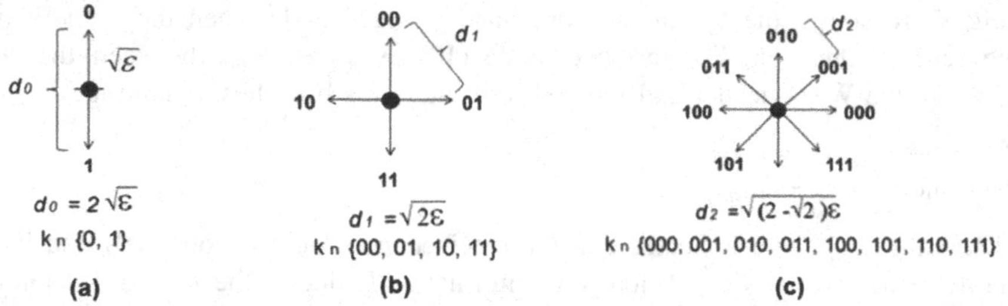

Fig. 2. Configurations of nodes and their respective d_{free} between the symbols of the sequence $k_n(t)$, with $d_0 > d_1 > d_2$. (a) Trellis node corresponding to the sequence set $k_n(t) = \{0, 1\}$; (b) Trellis node corresponding to the sequence set $k_n(t) = \{00, 01, 10, 11\}$; (c) Trellis node corresponding to the sequence set $k_n(t) = \{000, 001, 010, 011, 100, 101, 110, 111\}$.

An example of MM configuration proposed by Ungerboek [14] as shown in Fig. 3(a), represents a MM with rate k/n = 2/3, where the sequence $k_n(t)$ is composed of words with $v = 2$ symbols: $\{u_1u_2\}$ moving in the registers of MM with outputs $\{n_1n_2n_3\}$, resulting in a increase in the nodes connection capacity as shown by the equivalent trellis of the MM considered, Fig. 3(b). An important result in this configuration is the increase in the ability to establish routes on the trellis and the consequent time reduction of the trellis stabilization, which means to reach the *steady state* in fewer steps.

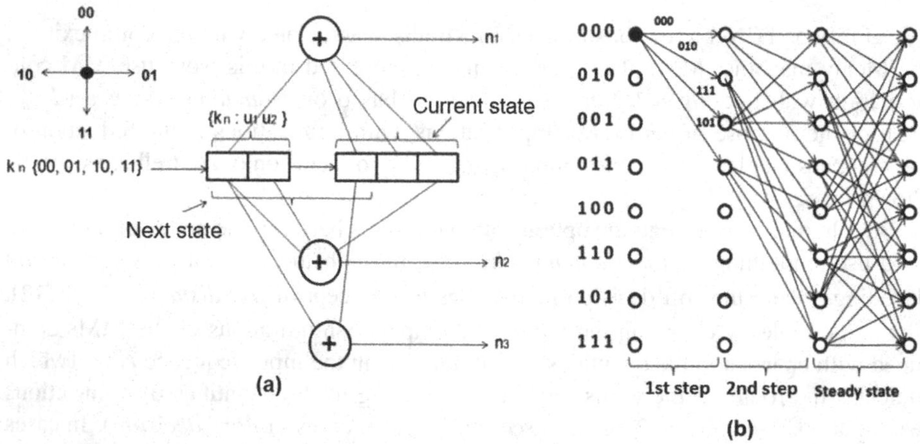

Fig. 3. (a) Configuration of the MM with rate k/n = 2/3, showing detail of node connection capacity; (b) The resulting trellis diagram with $2^v = 4$ branches connecting the nodes of the trellis and the instant that the trellis reaches the *steady state*.

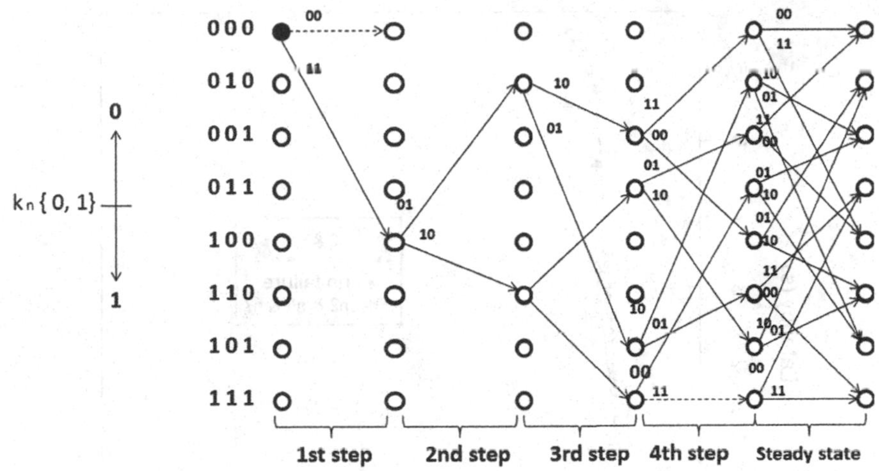

Fig. 4. Configuration of the trellis generated by the MM with rate k/n = 1/2 showing *steady state* after 4 th step.

3.2 Simulation Scenario with Network Nodes Failures Considering the Same Coverage Area

The initial scenario uses a MM with rate k/n = 1/2 and a sequence $k_n(t) = \{1\ 0\ 1\ 1\ 1\ 0\ 0\ 0\}$ defined by a desired QoS. Shifting the input sequence k_n *(t)* in the MM enables the reachability in a standard 8 node network, so that comparisons can be made in situations of nodes failures. In this simulation will be considered the nodes failures before the trellis reaches the *steady state*, due to the reasons presented in the first steps of trellis construction shown in Fig. 4:

- 1st step: Node *(100)* is required for the route initialization;
- 2nd step: Nodes *(010)* and *(110)* are used for trellis initialization, and failure may occur only in one of the nodes;
- 3rd step: Nodes *(001)*, *(011)*, *(101)* and *(111)* are also used for trellis initialization and, only two nodes can fail at the same time.

This work uses as simulation environment the OMNeT++ based on C++ and object oriented [15]. It has been chosen because it is an open software with applications in simulations and modeling of traffic networks, used as reference for comparisons among other techniques due to available frameworks.

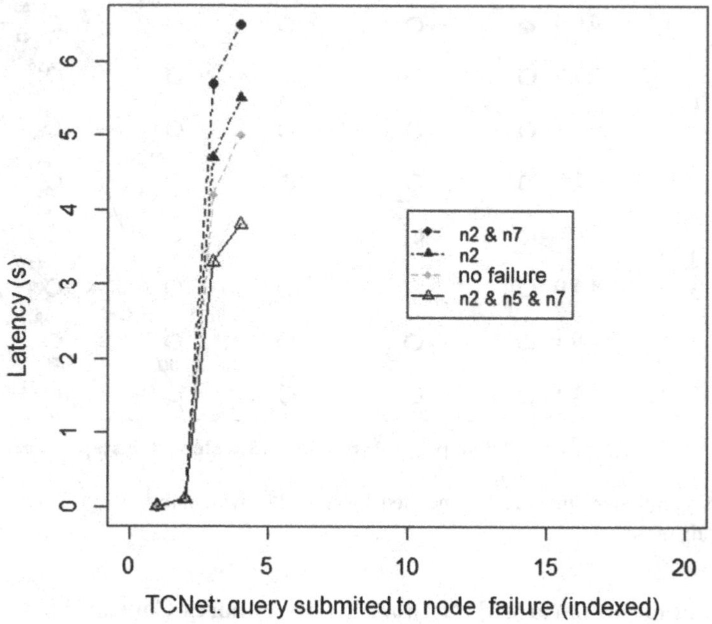

Fig. 5. Network latency resulting during route recovery, in failure cases: 1 node, 2 nodes and 3 nodes.

3.3 Cases of Nodes Failure in a 8 Nodes Network During a Query

The methodology used in this work to measure the efficiency of a network in the presence of node failures will be shown through latency during route recovery. In order to obtain the network latency during a query, the following data were normalized:

- Processing time $(t_p n)$, considered during data displacement in the MM;
- Channel delay (t_c), propagation time in the wireless communications channel considered;
- Guard band (t_g), time interval considered by the nodes between the multicasts of the FRAMES;
- Time out (t_{out}), time the network waits for the response of the requested node to decide to replace it by another network node.

Considering a theoretical scenario, with random distribution of the nodes in a coverage area with the maximum radius distance (dmax = 1000 m), Eq. (1) was used to evaluate the total latency of the network for the case of node failure:

$$\Sigma T_{Lf} = t_{pn} + t_c + t_g + t_{out} \tag{1}$$

In the considered scenario of nodes failures, the nodes to fail were chosen among those that compromise the trellis recovery. The nodes located in the first steps of the trellis, region of instability, were the chosen nodes in simulation environment below, as shown in Fig. 4:

- One node failure: node – *(010)* or **{2}** in 2 nd step of the trellis path;
- Two simultaneous nodes failures: node – *(010)* or **{2}** and node – *(111)* or **{7}** located in 3rd and 4th steps of the trellis path;
- Three simultaneous nodes failures: node – *(010)* or **{2}**, node – *(101)* or **{5}** and node – *(111)* or **{7}** in 2nd, 3rd and 4th steps of the trellis path;

Figure 5 shows the latency results to recover routes in cases of node failures, taking as reference a route without node failure as commented below:

- In case of one node failure, it results in a 10% increase in latency in relation to the network without node failure, due mainly to the (t_{out}) considered in the simulation;
- In case of 2 - nodes failures, it results in a 25% increase in latency in relation to the network without node failure;
- In case of 3 - nodes failures, it is important to realize that there was a reduction of the network by 50%, and even so the network recovers and completes the query with 70% of the latency of the network without any node failure.

3.4 Cases of Nodes Failure in Extended Networks During a Query

Considering the basic configuration of MM used in this work (Mealy machine with rate k/n = 1/2, Fig. 1(a)) and progressively adding shift registers and connections in its "XOR" gates, it is possible to generate higher densities networks which can be used to compare TCNet efficiency measures.

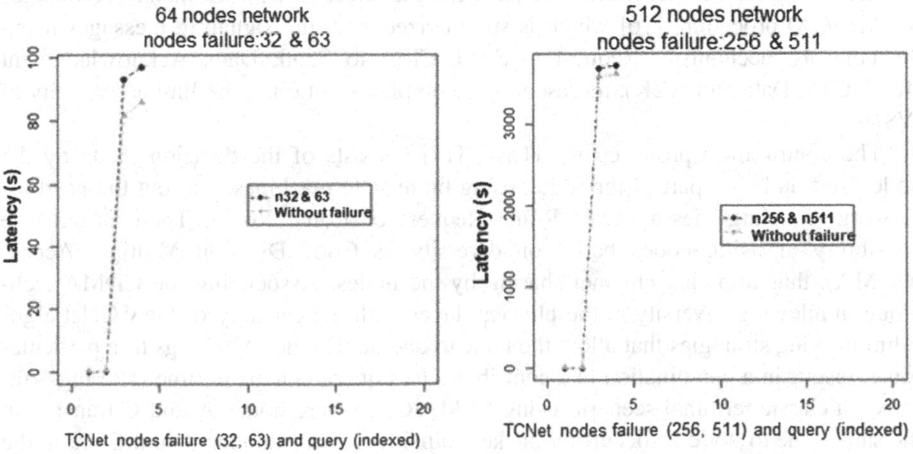

Fig. 6. Latency comparison in route recovery for networks with higher node density, with respect to the routes without failure considering two cases of increased networks.

Table 1. Latencies comparison in route recovery, as the nodes density increases.

Network	Nodes failure	Latency increase
16 nodes	n8 & n15	20%
32 nodes	n16 & n31	18.8%
64 nodes	n32 & n63	12.5%
128 nodes	n64 & n127	7.3%
256 nodes	n128 & n255	5.3%
512 nodes	n256 & n511	2.7%

The nodes selected for the case of failure in the higher density networks were chosen in the first steps of the trellis, (instability region of trellis). The results shown in Fig. 6 refer to the latencies comparison in route recovery, as the nodes density increases, with respect to the routes without failure, considering two cases of increasing network density: 64 nodes network and 512 nodes network.

Table 1 shows a progressive reduction of latency during route recovery, using the simulation environment [15], as the number of nodes increases in the network, considering more cases, making easier the trellis recovery.

3.5 Simulation Scenarios with Packet Collision

The main challenges in designing a routing algorithm for ad hoc networks according to [13], besides the problems related to: randomness of nodes and resource containment they are the hidden and exposed terminal. The hidden terminal contributes to the degradation of the data rate transfer in the network due to collisions caused and the terminal exposed is the existence of nodes belonging to the network but that are outside the coverage area. The practice adopted by the conventional protocols to overcome the problem consists of the Carrier Sense Multiple Access with Collision Avoidance (CSMA/CA) procedure [16] which is summarized with the signaling messages using the controls mechanism: Request to Send, Clear to Send, Data, Acknowledgment (RTS, CTS, Data and ACK), representing a complex solution to the limited capacity of WSNs.

The contribution proposed by TCNet [17] consists of the decision made by the node itself, in being part of the route, using finite state machines, without the need for network signaling messages as: Route Request or Route Reply. There is still the possibility of using codes based on diversity as Code Division Multiple Access (CDMA), thus allowing channel sharing by the nodes. Associating the CDMA technique in allowing diversity at the physical layer with the capacity of the TCNet algorithm in using strategies that allow the node to decide whether it belongs to a particular route, results in a combination that contributes to a query at a given time. The Fig. 7(a) shows a classic terminal scenario using CSMA/CA, where nodes A and C transmit at the same time to node B, occurring packet collision, because nodes A and C are in the hidden state of each other. The channel sharing solution involves the use of diversity at the physical layer level using Code Division Multiple Access (CDMA) as shown in Fig. 7(b). The solution adopted by TCNet uses the decision concept taken by the node

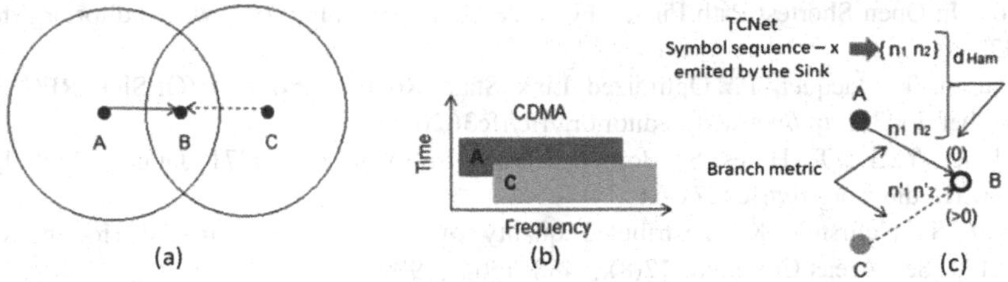

Fig. 7. (a) Scenario of hidden terminal using decision (CSMA/CA); (b) CDMA enabling them to share the same channel for packages A and C; (c) Mechanism of TCNet decision.

itself, based on the algorithm of Viterbi explained in [11], decoding the received sequence and estimating the minimum Hamming distance between the symbols of the sequence sent by Sink and the weight of the path branches as shown in Fig. 7(c).

Another possible collision scenario in ad hoc networks is the existence of nodes belonging to the network, but outside the coverage area, thus configuring the case of the exposed terminal. The TCNet scenarios are usually applied to hundreds of nodes distributed over large areas, suggesting in these cases the subdivision of these areas into *clusters*. In light of this, we propose in future works, studies of cases where scenarios with node *clusters* will be presented in order to solve packet collision.

4 Conclusions and Future Works

In this work it was reviewed the innovative approach of TCNet model introduced by the authors in [11] which exploits the new concept of route discovery quite advantageous for limited resources networks as is the case of WSNs.

It was shown the robustness of the process in case of nodes failures, and proposing solutions in cases of hidden and exposed nodes due to the packet collision problem in WSNs. In future works we intend to: (i) present results of efficiency of the process using *cluster* of nodes to solve packet collision and; (ii) to verify which extensions should be incorporated into RPL so that it can work according to the TCNet paradigm.

References

1. Sivalingam, K.M.: Tutorial on wireless sensor network protocols. In: International Conference on High Performance Computing 2002, Bangalore, India, December 2002
2. Perkins, C., Belding Royer, E., Das, S.: Ad hoc on - demand distance vector - (AODV) routing, RFC 3561, July 2003. http://www.rfc-editor.org/rfc/rfc3561.txt
3. RPL: IPv6 Routing Protocol for Low - Power and Lossy Networks. https://tools.ietf.org/html/rfc6550. Accessed 8 May 2018
4. Hendric, C.L.: Routing Information Protocol, RFC 1058, June 1988. http://www.rfc-editororg/rfc/rfc1058.txt
5. Oran, D.: OSI IS-IS Intra domain Routing Protocol, RFC 1141, February 1990. http://tools.Ietf.org/html/rfc1142

6. Moy, J.: Open Shortest Path First, RFC 2328, April 1988. http://www.rfc-editor.org/rfc/rfc.2328.txt
7. Clausen, T., Jacquet, P.: Optimized Link State Routing Protocol (OLSR), RFC 3626, October 2003. http://www.rfc-editor.org/rfc/rfc3626.txt
8. Rekhter, Y., Li, T., Hares, S.: Border Gateway Protocol, RFC 4271, January 2006. http://www.rfceditor.org/rfc/rfc4271.txt
9. Chen, S., Nahrsted, K.: Distributed quality of service routing in Ad Hoc networks. IEEE J. Sel. Areas Commun. **17**(8), 1488–1504 (1999)
10. Vasseur, J.P., Dunkels, A.: Interconnecting Smart Objects with IP The Next internet, 1st edn. Morgan Kaufmann, San Francisco (2010)
11. Lima Filho, D.F., Amazonas, J.R.: A new algorithm and routing protocol based on convolutional codes using TCNet: Trellis Coded Network. In: The 1st EAI International Conference on Smart Grid Assisted Internet of Things – SGIoT/2017. Springer. ISBN 978-1-63190-152-2. http://eudl.eu/proceedings/SGIoT/2017
12. Proakis, J.G., Salehi, M.: Digital Communications, 5th edn. Mc Graw Hill, New York (2008)
13. Fullmer, C.L., Garcia, J.J.: Solutions to hidden terminal problems in wireless netwoks. In: Proceedings of ACM SIGCOMM 1997, pp. 39–49, September 1997
14. Biglieri, E., Divsalar, D., Mclane, P.J., Simon, M.K.: Introduction to Trellis - Code Modulation with Applications. Macmillan Publishing Company, New York (1991)
15. Varga, A.: OMNeT++ Discrete Event Simulation System (2011). http://www.omnetpp
16. Nasipuri, A., Zhuang, J., Das, S.R.: A Multi-channel CSMA MAC protocol for multi-hop wireless networks. In: Proceedings of IEEE WCNC (1999)
17. Lima Filho, D.F., Amazonas, J.R: A Trellis Coded Networks-based approach to solve the hidden and exposed nodes problems in WSNs. In: Segundo Seminário Taller Latinoamericano de Instumentación Control y Telecomunicaciones, Proceedings of SICOTEL, p. 297 (2014). ISBN 978-958-8593-44-9

Applications and Technologies

Effectiveness of Hard Clustering Algorithms for Securing Cyber Space

Sakib Mahtab Khandaker[1,2(✉)], Afzal Hussain[1,2], and Mohiuddin Ahmed[1,2]

[1] Islamic University of Technology, Gazipur City, Bangladesh
{sakibmahtab,afzalhussain}@iut-dhaka.edu,
m.ahmed.au@ieee.org

[2] Canberra Institute of Technology, Reid, Australia

Abstract. In the era of big data, it is more challenging than before to accurately identify cyber attacks. The characteristics of big data create constraints for the existing network anomaly detection techniques. Among these techniques, unsupervised algorithms are superior than the supervised algorithms for not requiring training data. Among the unsupervised techniques, hard clustering is widely accepted for deployment. Therefore, in this paper, we investigated the effectiveness of different hard clustering techniques for identification of a range of state-of-the-art cyber attacks such as *backdoor, fuzzers, worms, reconnaissance* etc. from the popular UNSW-NB15 dataset. The existing literature only provides the accuracy of identification of the all types of attacks in generic fashion, however, our investigation ensures the effectiveness of hard clustering for individual attacks. The experimental results reveal the performance of a number of hard clustering techniques. The insights from this paper will help both the cyber security and data science community to design robust techniques for securing cyber space.

Keywords: Network traffic analysis · Cyber attacks
Unsupervised clustering · Big data

1 Introduction

Technology have been increasing at breakneck speed and with it the amount of data generated thus the word big data has become ubiquitous in both academic and industrial domains. Although it is a relatively new term which was only coined in 2008 [2], it became a buzzword after the Mckinsley Global Institute report [3] but there still remains confusion as to the amount of data denoted by it. Big data is the driving force behind many digital transformation waves like internet of things, data science and artificial intelligence. The term can properly be defined using the "5V" – volume (referring to the large amount of data requiring no traditional processing methods), velocity (the high speed at which data is produced), variety (denoting the structured, semi structured and unstructured form of generated data), veracity (the quality of the data)

A.-S. K. Pathan et al. (Eds.): SGIoT 2018, LNICST 256, pp. 113–120, 2019.
https://doi.org/10.1007/978-3-030-05928-6_11

and value (referring to the added value big data brings) [1]. By reflecting on all existing definitions, Big data has been [4] defined as *"Big Data represents the Information assets characterized by such a High Volume, Velocity and Variety to require specific Technology and Analytical Methods for its transformation into Value."* Use of big data implies dealing with large amount of structured, unstructured and semi structured data ranging from petabytes, exabytes to even yotabytes [5]. Big data comes with a cost, it creates information security and privacy breach but big data analytics on the other hand promises detection and prevention of such cyber attacks. Real time analysis of patterns, outlier detection and attack recognition through correlation and machine learning is where big data analysis can play a big role in cyber security. Big data holds the key to solve information security threat by providing real time actionable insights [6]. Extension of traditional security and real time large scale analysis, compassion, anomaly detection of heterogeneous data sets at greater speed have been made possible with the newer big data technologies like Hadoop ecosystem, stream mining, complex-event processing and NoSQL databases [7].

The contribution of this paper lies in the fact that 3 different unsupervised algorithms were used here for anomaly detection namely - kmeans, kmedoids and kmodes. We used them to identify different types of cyber attacks like - analysis, exploits, reconnaissance, worms, backdoor, fuzzers, shellcode, DoS and generic attacks. Among the three, kmodes showed the highest accuracy with an overall accuracy of 69%. It was able to segregate different types of cyber attacks from the UNSW-NB15 dataset which is used as a standard for cyber security research. This paper sheds light on the potential of unsupervised algorithms in cyber security.

1.1 Roadmap

The Rest of the paper is organized as follows: Sect. 2 discusses about different network anomaly techniques then Sect. 3 focuses on hard clustering algorithms. In Sect. 4 different types of cyber attacks are described. Finally experimental results are highlighted in Sect. 5 and Sect. 6 is where we draw the conclusion.

2 Network Anomaly Detection Techniques

Anomaly detection can be referred to the detection of nonconforming patterns in regular data. These abnormal data are sometimes termed as outliers, exceptions, peculiarities or contaminants in different paradigm. The most common terms used terms are anomaly and outlier. Actionable intelligence anomaly detection provides where its most importance lies. Outlier or anomaly detection can be dated back to the 19th century [8]. Some of the challenges which come up when detecting outliers keeping up with constantly evolving normal behavior, availability of labeled data for training or validation and often data contains noise which gives rise to false positives [9]. Compared to statistical approach which focuses on understanding the process of data generation, machine learning focuses on providing the necessary answer based on previous available data thus creating a dynamic system with adaptive capability. Now machine learning based anomaly detection can be divided into three categories - supervised, semi supervised and unsupervised.

Supervised anomaly detection presumes that training data set is available with labeling denoting normal and anomalous instances. The usual approach for such a method is build a predictive model of normal vs anomaly. New data entries are compared with preexisting ones to determine its position among the two cases. Sadly this method has drawbacks. Firstly the training data set contains fewer anomalous incidents compared to normal ones. Secondly obtaining accurate and suitable labels especially in case of anomaly is difficult.

Semi supervised techniques work with the presumption that training data has been labeled for normal instances. As anomalous instances are not labeled here its add flexibility to their application. There are a few number of semi supervised techniques which assumes availability of anomalous cases [10,11]. But these techniques are less used because of the fact that obtaining training data set for all anomalous cases is not possible.

Lastly we have unsupervised anomaly detection technique where there id no need of a training data set. Such techniques make two implicit assumptions. First, the major part of the data set is constituted of normal cases and only a small percentage are anomalies and the other assumptions is that anomalous cases are statistically different from normal cases.

Application of unsupervised algorithm for cyber security has gained momentum in academic paradigm. The accuracy and effectiveness of fixed width clustering, optimized k nearest neighbor support vector machine have been shown in Eskin et al. [12]. Old - meadow et al. showed improvement of cluster accuracy when the said clusters are adaptive [13]. A two tier novel intrusion detection system was proposed in by Zanero et al. [14]. Phad et al. examines IP headers connections to various ports as well as packet headers of Ethernet, IP and transport layers packet headers [15]. Alad et al. detects anomalies in inbound TCP connections to well known ports on the server [16]. Lerad et al. detects TCP stream anomalies like alad but uses a learning algorithm to pick good rules from training set rather than using a fixed set of rules [17]. K-mean was used by Dragon Research and Nairac for novelty detection [18,19]. Gaddam et al. showed a method to detect anomalous activities using k means clustering [20].

3 Hard Clustering

When it comes to the taxonomy of clustering algorithms we can categorize them into two broad groups as shown in Fig. 1. Hierarchical clustering algorithms can either be successive splitting (divisive) or merging (agglomerative) of groups to form a hierarchy based on similarity or a specific measure of distance. Hierarchical algorithms can also be sub classified according to the process the distances or similarities between objects are updated after splitting or merging groups. On the other hand partitional clustering algorithms focus on portioning data based

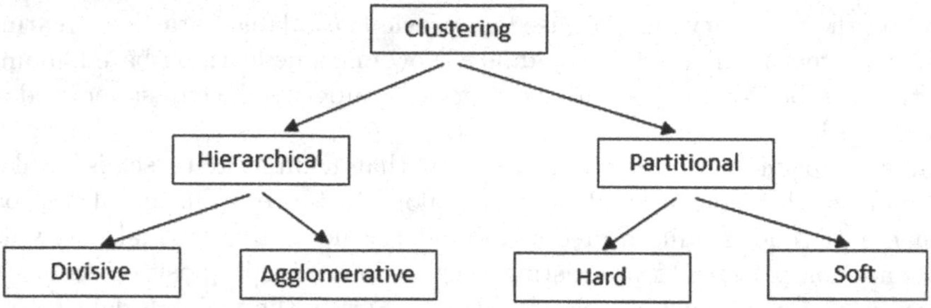

Fig. 1. Taxonomy of clustering algorithm

on distance between objects. On further classification we have hard and soft clustering. A hard clustering algorithm allocates each pattern to a single cluster and no data points is assigned to two clusters while soft clustering assigns degrees of member in several cluster to each input pattern.

The field of cyber security requires a clear distinction between normal cases and anomalous cases. Hard clustering was more suitable for such application. We have evaluated the performance of three hard clustering algorithms- k-means, k-modes and k-medoid for identification of different types of cyber attacks.

4 Attack Description

We have used the UNSW-NB 15 data set for our experiment [21]. A short description of the attacks found in this data set has been described [22].

1. Fuzzer: is a type of attack when the attacker attempts to exploit weakness of a security system by forcing it to crash by providing larger quantities of random data.
2. Analysis: combination of multifarious intrusion techniques including penetration of ports, email address and even web scripts.
3. Backdoor: Such type of attack attempts to bypass the authentication thus allowing unauthorized remote access.
4. DoS: This type of attack overloads memory to a state of unresponsiveness
5. Exploit: A series of instructions designed to work around vulnerabilities of the system from bugs to glitches.
6. Generic: Uses functions to cause collision of block ciphers.
7. Reconnaissance: a probe that attempts to gather information necessary to exploit security weakness.
8. Shellcode: An attack where a simple injection of command into the running system leads to full control of the system.
9. Worm: A replication based attack where the attacker replicates itself into multiple hosts.

5 Experimental Analysis

In order to evaluate the performance of the machine learning algorithms we have used confusion matrix [23]. The confusion matrix has four cells as shown in Table 1, True Positive (TP) which shows the number of attacks detected, True Negative (TN) which shows the number of normal instances detected, False Positive (FP) showing false alarms and False Negative (FN) where the algorithm mistakes an attack for normal case.

To find the accuracy we have used the formula:

$$\frac{TN + TF}{TN + TF + FP + FN} \tag{1}$$

We have evaluated the accuracy of all three algorithms for each type of attacks as shown in Table 2.

The dataset used here is the UNSW-15 which was created using an IXIA Perfectstorm tool in the Cyber Range Lab of the Australian Centre for Cyber Security (ACCS) to generate a set of realistic normal cyber activities and synthetic contemporary attack behaviors. Through the use of a tcpdump tool 100 GB of raw network traffic with a total of 2,540,044 records.

We applied the algorithms on each type of attacks for different split to find accuracy as shown in Fig. 2. It has been found that among the three algorithms kmodes showed the highest accuracy for all types of attacks with an overall average of 70% followed by kmedoid which had an average of 63% for cyber attack detection. The performance of all the algorithms for different split ratios have also been shown in Fig. 2 for better understanding of their performance.

Table 1. Confusion matrix

	Negative	Positive
Actual negative	TN	FP
Actual positive	FN	TP

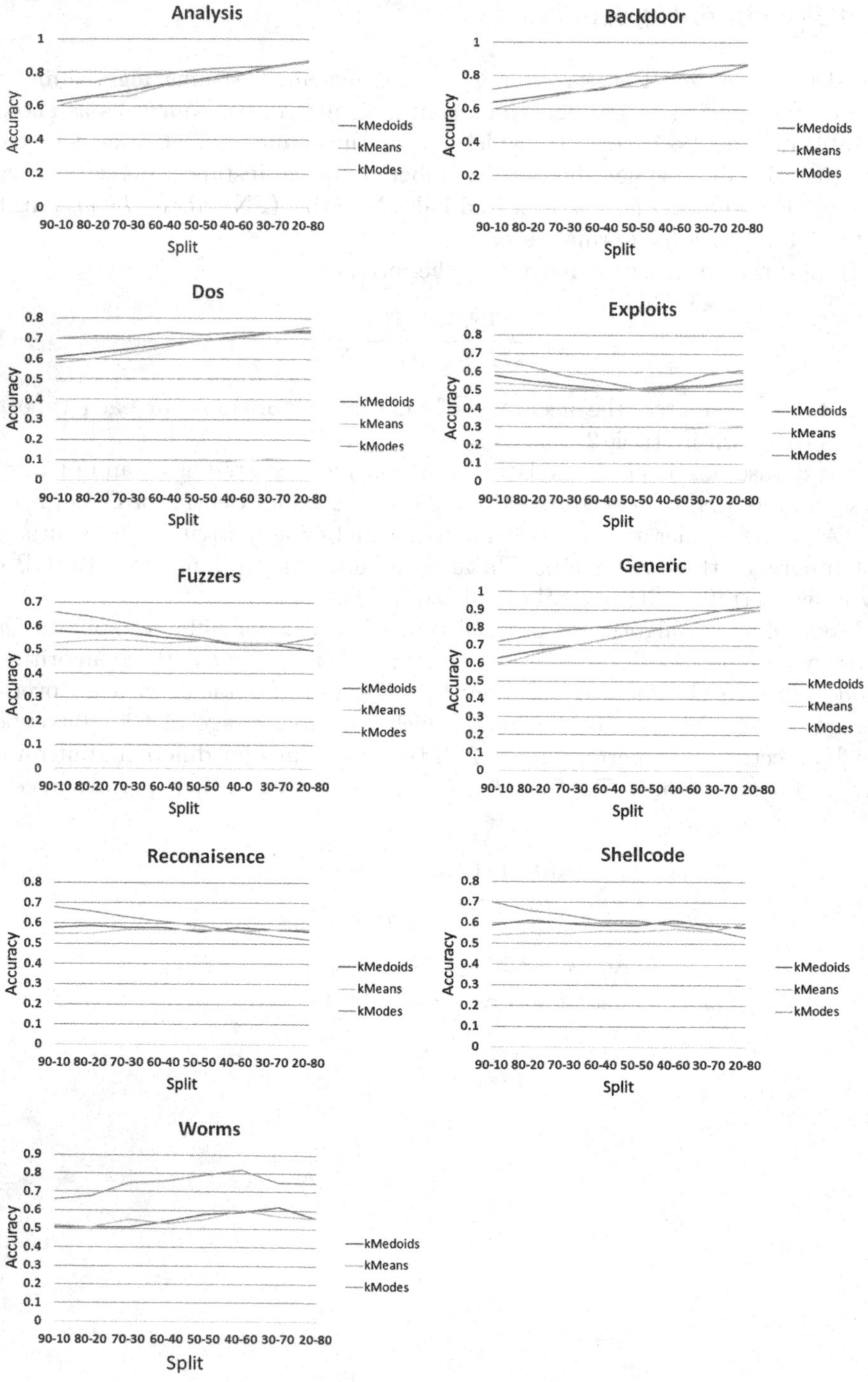

Fig. 2. Accuracy of algorithms

Table 2. Accuracy of different algorithms

	kmedoid	kmean	kmodes
Analysis	0.74625	0.73125	0.80125
Exploits	0.535	0.51875	0.58375
Reconaisence	0.575	0.56375	0.59875
Worms	0.5525	0.54875	0.745
Backdoor	0.745	0.73625	0.79875
Fuzzers	0.54375	0.5325	0.5775
Shellcode	0.595	0.56125	0.61375
DoS	0.67875	0.66875	0.72
Generic	0.7625	0.755	0.825
Overall avg.	0.637083	0.624028	0.695972

6 Conclusions and Future Research

In this paper, we investigated the performance of unsupervised approaches to identify different types of network attacks. From our experimental analysis, we come to a conclusion that the k-modes clustering algorithm outperforms the k-means and k-medoid algorithms in terms of accurately identifying nine different types of cyber attacks from the state-of-the-art datasets. We have used different combination to avoid any bias in our investigation and it turns out that k-modes algorithm consistently performs better than the rest. In future we are going to address the issue of automatic centroid calculation and mixed type of attributes in the datasets.

References

1. Baaziz, A., Quoniam, L.: How to use Big Data technologies to optimize operations in Upstream Petroleum Industry. Int. J. Innov. **1**(1), 19–29 (2013)
2. Editorial: community cleverness required. Nature **455**(7209), 1 (2008). http://www.nature.com/news/specials/bigdata/index.html
3. Manyika, J., et al.: Big Data: The Next Frontier for Innovation, Competition, and Productivity. McKinsey Global Institute, New York (2011)
4. De Mauro, A., Greco, M., Grimaldi, M.: What is big data? A consensual definition and a review of key research topics. In: AIP Conference Proceedings, vol. 1644, pp. 97–104. AIP (2015). http://aip.scitation.org/doi/abs/10.1063/1.4907823
5. Akerkar, R.: Big Data Computing, International Standard Book Number 13: 978-1-4665-7838-8
6. Mahmood, T., Afzal, U.: Security analytics: big data analytics for cybersecurity: a review of trends, techniques and tools. In: 2013 2nd National Conference on Information Assurance (NCIA), Rawalpindi, pp. 129–134 (2013)
7. Alguliyev, R., Imamverdiyev, Y.: Big data: big promises for information security. In: Proceedings of the 2014 8th IEEE International Conference on Application of Information and Communication Technology AICT, pp. 1–4, October 2014

8. Edgeworth, F.Y.: On discordant observations. Philosoph. Mag. **23**(5), 364–375 (1887)
9. Chandola, V., Banerjee, A., Kumar, V.: Anomaly detection. ACM Comput. Sur. **41**(3), 1–58 (2009). https://doi.org/10.1145/1541880.1541882
10. Dasgupta, D., Andmajumdar, N.: Anomaly detection in multidimensional data using negative selection algorithm. In: Proceedings of the IEEE Conference on Evolutionary Computation, pp. 1039–1044 (2002)
11. Dasgupta, D., Andnino, F.: A comparison of negative and positive selection algorithms in novel pattern detection. Proc. IEEE Int. Conf. Syst. Man Cybernet. **1**, 125–130 (2000)
12. Eskin, E., Arnold, A., Prerau, M., Portnoy, L., Stolfo, S.: A geometric framework for un-supervised anomaly detection: detecting intrusions in unlabeled data. In: Barbará, D., Jajodia, S. (eds.) Applications of Data Mining in Computer Security, vol. 6. Springer, Boston (2002). https://doi.org/10.1007/978-1-4615-0953-0_4
13. Oldmeadow, J., Ravinutala, S., Leckie, C.: Adaptive clustering for network intrusion detection. In: Dai, H., Srikant, R., Zhang, C. (eds.) PAKDD 2004. LNCS, vol. 3056, pp. 255–259. Springer, Heidelberg (2004). https://doi.org/10.1007/978-3-540-24775-3_33
14. Zanero, S., Savaresi, S.: Unsupervised learning techniques for an intrusion detection system. In: Proceedings of the ACM Symposium on Applied Computing, SAC 2004. ACM (2004)
15. Mahoney, M.V., Chan, P.K.: PHAD: Packet Header Anomaly Detection for Identifying Hostile Network Traffic Department of Computer Sciences, Florida Institute of Technology, Melbourne, FL, USA, Technical report CS- 2001-4, April 2001
16. Mahoney, M.V., Chan, P.K.: Learning nonstationary models of normal network traffic for detecting novel attacks. In: Proceedings of the Eighth ACM SIGKDD International Conference on Knowledge Discovery and Data Mining, Edmonton, Canada, pp. 376–385 (2002)
17. Mahoney, M.V., Chan, P.K.: Learning Models of Network Traffic for Detecting Novel Attacks Computer Science Department, Florida Institute of Technology CS-2002-8, August 2002
18. Allan, J., Carbonell, J., Doddington, G., Yamron, J., Yang, Y.: Topic detection and tracking pilot study: final report. In: Proceedings of the DARPA Broadcast News Transcription and Understanding Workshop (1998)
19. Nairac, A., Townsend, N., Carr, R., King, S., Cowley, P., Tarassenko, L.: A system for the analysis of jet system vibration data. Integr. Comput. Aided Eng. **6**(1), 53–65 (1999)
20. Gaddam, S.R., Phoha, V.V., Balagani, K.S.: K-Means+ID3: a novel method for supervised anomaly detection by cascading K-means clustering and ID3 decision tree learning methods. IEEE Trans. Knowl. Data Eng. **19**(3), 345–354 (2007)
21. Moustafa, N., Slay, J.: UNSW-NB15 DataSet for Network Intrusion Detection Systems, May 2014. http://www.cybersecurity.unsw.adfa.edu.au/ADFA20NB15
22. Moustafa, N., Slay, J.: The evaluation of Network Anomaly Detection Systems: statistical analysis of the UNSW-NB15 data set and the comparison with the KDD99 data set. Inf. Secur. J. Glob. Perspect. **25**(1–3), 18–31 (2016)
23. Fawcett, T.: An introduction to ROC analysis. Pattern Recogn. Lett. **27**, 861–874 (2006). https://doi.org/10.1016/j.patrec.2005.10.010

On Data Driven Organizations and the Necessity of Interpretable Models

Tony Lindgren(✉)

Department of Computer and System Sciences, Stockholm University, Borgarfjordsgatan 12, 164 40 Kista, Sweden
tony@dsv.su.se

Abstract. It this paper we investigate data driven organizations in the context of predictive models, we also reflect on the need for interpretability of the predictive models in such a context. By investigating a specific use-case, the maintenance offer from a heavy truck manufacturer, we explore their current situation trying to identify areas that needs change in order to go from the current situation towards a more data driven and agile maintenance offer. The suggestions for improvements are captured in a proposed data driven framework for this type of business. The aim of the paper is that the suggested framework can inspire and start further discussions and investigations into the best practices for creating a data driven organization, in businesses facing similar challenges as in the presented use-case.

Keywords: Data driven framework · Interpretability · Organization

1 Introduction

As organizations such as governments, corporations, educational institutions (from here on referred to as organizations), start to re-organize their work with the intent to harness and utilize the data that they are (or could be) in possession of, they are confronted with different challenges. One can partition the challenges into two major themes, technical and organizational. The technical challenges can include how to efficiently collect data, how to store it, how to query and analyze it etc. On the organizational level decisions on which department will do what and their responsibiltes must be made. Typically, the end goal for an organization that have initiated change in the above mentioned direction is to "become data driven". The silent assumption is that a data driven organization is the pinnacle of efficiency, with very low waste, be it in time, effort or any other scares resource [10].

One organizational model that subscribes to this data driven organizational idea is the New Public Management (NPM) [2], which strives to generate feedback loops which can be used to guide the organization. These feedback loops have become more common everywhere in society. It can materialize itself in

A.-S. K. Pathan et al. (Eds.): SGIoT 2018, LNICST 256, pp. 121–130, 2019.
https://doi.org/10.1007/978-3-030-05928-6_12

the form of survey machines at the supermarket or after you rented a car you will receive an e-mail or text-message from a survey firm with questions. Some organizations have this feedback loop tightly coupled to their business model, for example Airbnb and Uber, while others like Facebook and Google tries to get feedback from your GPS data to be able to make better recommendations in the future. In Fig. 1 two examples of creating feedback is shown. There have been quite a few attempts to formalize the activities and the different steps needed to successfully create data driven organizations, these descriptions come at different abstraction levels, from practical and concrete descriptions of the process steps needed to facilitate analysis of data [9] to suggestions on how to organize work [10]. One aspect of becoming a data driven organization is the acceptance and utilization of abstractions and inferences made from the data provided both by the explicit feedback-loop and other data relevant to the service provided by the organization. Data science and data mining is the study of how to, from data, create such abstractions which typically involve the process of searching for patterns or regularities in data and then describing these regularities through a predictive model. Predictive models have been put into use by organizations more frequently in recent years, and is one of the reasons for the increased interest in the area of model interpretability. For a good overview of this area the reader is encouraged to read [7]. In this paper we are interested in the interpretability of inductive models and how this feature fit into the concept of data driven organizations.

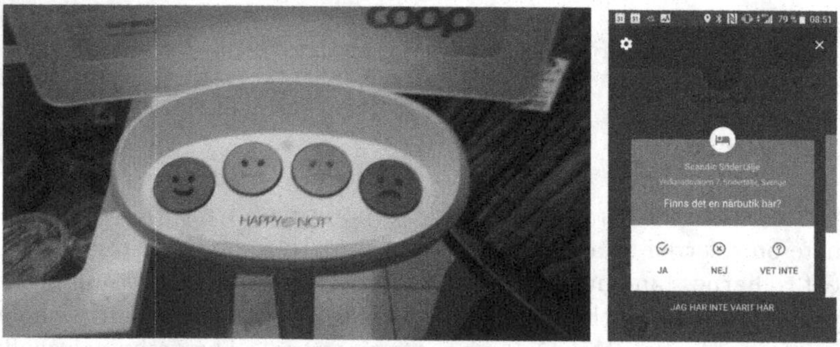

(a) (b)

Fig. 1. A few examples for creating a feedback loop

The rest of the paper is structured as follows: first we will look into the life-cycles of inductive models in data driven organizations, then we will look into the role of interpretability for inductive models. We will then present our use-case and its problems then present a data driven framework which addresses these problems. Finally, we finish off the paper with a discussion about the proposed framework.

2 Life Cycle of Inductive Models in Data Driven Organizations

One of the most commonly referenced process for doing data mining is the *CRoss-Industry Standard Process for Data Mining* (CRISP-DM) [9]. CRISP-DM divides the data mining process into six different phases. The phases are: business understanding, data understanding, data preparation, modelling, (model) evaluation, and (model) deployment. Business understanding include the major steps of understanding the business objectives for initializing the data mining effort and converting this knowledge into a data mining problem and designing a plan to reach the business objectives. Data understanding, data preparation and modelling are all phases which are instrumental to the specific data mining task. Model evaluation are important as this step checks whether or not the business objectives are fulfilled by the inductive model. The next step is to proceed into the deployment phase, if the objectives are fulfilled. CRISP-DM does not touch upon how work should or could be organized to facilitate the suggested process phases. One can also argue that CRISP-DM put very limited emphasis on the steps after deployment.

Traditionally organizations have been organized in a hierarchical fashion, where different parallel organizations have had different functions, be it research and development, production, aftermarket, customer relations etc. Still this way of organizing work is common. Difficulties which have been identified with such a structure is that such organizations can be slow to react upon changes in its environment, and that cross functional work can be hindered [1]. This has led to the advent of organizations which focus on the process or in values streams to make them explicit and assign the responsibility of certain parts of the process to certain parts in the functional organization [3].

In their article [6], which focus on humans working in data driven organizations, and the impact this has on their working environment. The article investigates two ridesharing organizations, Uber and Lyft, in which the human jobs are assigned and evaluated by algorithms in a data driven framework. Both Lyft and Uber allow for few managers to, via algorithms manage thousands of drivers worldwide. In both companies the drivers log in to an application, typically on a mobile device, to signal that they are ready to receive jobs. Exactly how the algorithm matches vehicles and customers is secret in both cases but proximity is one of the factors.

Active drivers have a limited time (15 s in case of Uber) to accept a fare or not. Areas with many customers and few vehicles are signaled in the app, to encouraged drivers to go to this areas, as incentive drivers will receive a higher compensation (pay) for these fares. The drivers can be judged by their customers and the driver can also rate the passengers. The main feedback loop into the data driven system is the ratings and for drivers the percentage of accepted drives w.r.t. offered fares. The drivers also get payment promotions (each hour) if they are active for longer periods. All these variables can cause drivers, who have a good understanding of how the algorithm works to, for example, park between two other uber-cars while having lunch to make sure that they are still online but have a small risk of actually receiving a fare. Yet another consequence is that some drivers who don't want to take customers from a certain area turn off their application while passing through that area, to avoid having to pass on a fare.

The main findings in the study indicate that drivers were to some extent frustrated by the lack of transparency of why they were offered some fares even though they were not the closest, or being judged when they passed up fare even though they had a good reason for it. The authors of the study suggest that improving the transparency of the algorithm most probably would increase the acceptance and trust of the fare assignments, but also might come at the cost that more drivers will "know" how to exploit the algorithm.

Another type of data driven management is NPM, this has received criticism for just creating more bureaucracy and not have the good effects on steering the organization which was the original idea. Hoggett [4] provide one description of this problem:

"Excessive formalization has proved to be organizationally dysfunctional, creating new layers of bureaucracy engaged in contract specification and monitoring, quality control, inspection, audit and review and diverting the energies of professional staff away from service and program delivery into a regime of form-filling, report writing and procedure following which is arguably even more extensive than that which existed during the former bureaucratic era."

The above statement gives a good starting point to reflect on the roots of NPM which has been inspired by methods used in manufacturing industry for improving quality. The public sector and other organizations which are conducting more abstract and creative work might not readily adhere to the criteria's needed to successfully become data driven, as the tasks are not easily measured, and hence a good feedback loop is hard to envisage. Below follows yet another problem of NPM:

"It might sound paradoxical, but stressed and de-motivated, 'unable' and/or 'unwilling' employees fit quite well into the ideological framework of NPM. Such aspects underline the necessity of more policies and procedures, of more systematic performance measurement and appraisal, of more monitoring and advising, of more 'leadership' and 'motivation' - for the whole arsenal of managerial concepts and methods." in [5].

The two data driven organizations from the former paper, Uber and Lyft, can ignore the problem above as their workers are not employed by them and hence they can skip the motivation part and fire them (or, rather, ban them from using their app) if they do not follow their minimum criteria.

We conclude this section with a summary: it exists a lot of driving forces for organizations to become data driven, efficiency being one of the more important ones. As we have noted by the anecdotal NPM-quotations above, not all tasks within an organization can be easily transform into a data driven tasks. We will elaborate more upon which criterions are needed and/or sufficient for a successful data driven tasks creation in later sections.

3 Interpretability of Inductive Models

Interpretability of inductive models has recently attracted more attention, there might be many reasons for this, but one of the most important reasons is that the (actual or planned) usage of inductive models start to become more common in organizations. For each organization this can pose new opportunities and raise new questions, as we have seen earlier when models or algorithms manage workers it can be seen as both cold and in-humane, but it can also be seen as an opportunity as all workers is treated equal.

In his [7] overview paper of the area of interpretability he identifies that there is not clear technical definition for interpretability at the moment and that different researchers do put emphasis on different properties and aspects related to interpretability, be it: trust, causality, transferability, fair and ethical decisions. Demand for interpretability can come from the users of the model or by regulatory agencies for example General Data Protection Regulation (GDPR) in the EU, which include, the right for citizens to contest automatic profiling from algorithms. This implies that European citizens have the right to know and understand algorithmic decisions, which in turn, means that an explanation must be provided for a particular case together with a prediction of a model.

It might then not come as a surprise that new methods for facilitating interpretability for particular predictions have been devised lately. These methods typically produce an explanation for a particular classification by introducing a local explanation model as a mediator between the instance and the global model. One such method is Local Interpretable Model-agnostic Explanations (LIME) [8]. One way LIME present its explanation is by showing the support in favor of and against the prediction.

One example of a method for facilitating interpretability is described in the paper [11], here the authors aim not only to explain why a certain prediction is given on a certain instance, but they also investigate how (with minimal effort) to change the prediction output via features which can be adjusted. This type of explanation could be very important and one that we often (as humans) take for granted. For example, let's imagine that you go to the doctor and get a diagnosis that you will have a heart attack within six months, then you are told to go home. This information is not sufficient to be helpful for you. After given such a diagnosis you want to receive advice on the changeable features, i.e. factor you can affect to avoid being in the class of patients that you were diagnosed as.

As mentioned already one of the reasons of creating interpretable models is for establishing trust in the models, here the assumption is that if the models are understood then trust will emerge. But is the interpretability of models necessary? If we have a model that behaves as an oracle in that it always makes the correct prediction, do we then need an explanation for the predictions? I would believe that most humans eventually would accept the models predictions without needing further explanation due to the oracles previous results in successful predictions.

4 Use-Case and Proposed Framework

Here we will describe the use-case we have studied and then present a data driven framework for supporting the use-case.

4.1 Use-Case

In this case study we will look at the situation at a European based globally present manufacturer, OEM, of commercial vehicles. We will in this use-case focus on the maintenance offer by the OEM and the demands on it. Traditionally manufacturers of trucks and buses have sold their vehicles to fleet owners and also offered maintenance contracts for these vehicles. This is still the case, but there are plans to provide transportation (tonnage/km) or bus (operation/hours) as a service. By using such a service, the fleet owner shifts into a fleet operator. In this new business model, the fleet owner has to pay a fee for the transportation service and is in return guaranteed an uptime percentage, i.e. the time when the transportation service can be utilized. Downtime, when the transport service is unavailable, can be divided into planned downtime, and un-planned downtime. Minimizing or eliminating the un-planned downtime, i.e. typically when a vehicle has broken down, is desirable. Planned downtime could for example be when maintenance is conducted on the vehicle, if this can be planned in a flexible way, it can often be aligned with a time when the fleet operator does not need the transport service.

Transport as a service puts high demands on knowing the actual health status of a particular vehicle to avoid un-planned downtime. With the aim of providing more uptime and only planned downtime, the OEMs maintenance program have in the last couple of years gone from a fixed interval (km and/or hours) based maintenance program to a data driven maintenance program. In the new program, the models for expressing the maintenance needs for particular components are both induced by machine learning algorithms and created manually by experts. While the maintenance models created by experts do not needed to be interpreted (at least not by the experts them self), there is a need to simulate the consequences of their manual crafted rules, to be able to validate them on a bigger population. The maintenance experts have a production tool which supports creation of expert rules and the functionality to simulate these rules on the current population before putting them into production.

The models produced by machine learning methods are typically validated by both their performance metrics and by manual inspection of the models. The latter demand has put restrictions on the type of models which can be utilized, typically they should be transparent, i.e. not black boxes, and not too complex. These demands for simple models put limitations on the performance of the machine learning methods. As we have discussed earlier the feedback loops in data driven organizations is essential for these types of organizations to work properly. At the OEM the main feedback loop was designed to quickly be able to respond to quality issues w.r.t. sub-series of components etc. But this feedback loop has not yet been modified to align with the new maintenance program.

The transport service offer that the OEM makes towards potential customers is typically made by experienced sales personnel who together with the potential customer investigate the needs of transport service provided by the OEM. If the customer already owns a vehicle from the OEM then the data from previous operations can be used, for specifying which new product that would suit the customer best and also estimate the cost for the transport service offered to the customer. If the customer changes utilization of the transport service, the customer and the OEM needs to re-negotiate the terms of the customer offer.

4.2 Proposed Framework

Given the use-case we will now present a suggestion for a framework that will support data driven ambition for the maintenance offer, the framework is shown in Fig. 2. The framework is initialized to the left in the figure with the alignment of product development with model development. Each model is created for a specific component and should be able to with a high certainty predict when the component needs maintenance to avoid failure. If the model predicts need for maintenance (maintenance decision) before failure, the model is working correct, but can waste resources, feedback of changed components needs to be analyzed to make sure that components are not changed prematurely. If the model fails to predict correctly and a failure of the component do happen, its cause should be analyzed (analysis). The outcome of analysis could be: the model is valid, there is a need to set off the alarm to alert humans that the models needs attention. This might trigger a number of actions, one being the need for analyzing the problematic cases together with the model to understand the problem and refine the model by these findings to cope with similar cases in the future. Having presented the general framework, we investigate how we can improve the OEMs service offer using it, the first step is to integrate the creation of a data driven models as a natural step in the product development process (left in the figure), this is not the case at the OEM now. There have been efforts in this direction for certain components by individual maintenance experts and keen development engineers working together, but this work needs to be a mandatory step in the product development process. Questions like: Who will have responsibility of the maintenance prediction model over time? Who will create data driven models? When should Machine learning or other modelling techniques be used? Needs to be answered.

My suggestion is that for each new product development effort at the OEM, create a team of maintenance experts, data science experts and the development engineers. The first task of the team is to assess the impact of component failure from different viewpoints, be it road safety, fulfillment of transport service, environmental aspects, etc. These viewpoints would then serve as input into how much time, effort and money the team can use for creating prediction models. The most expensive model being a physical model hand-crafted by senior engineers and should only be constructed for very critical components. Data driven models are cheaper to create but they rely on historical data of failures. If data driven models are chosen, a plan for collecting data from test, be it from rigs, to

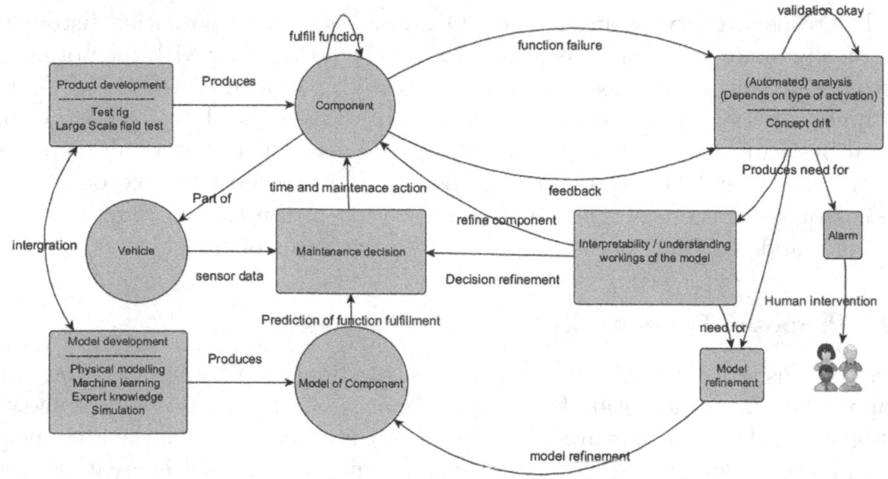

Fig. 2. A schematic view of the suggested framework

simulate usage, and later when the component is out in field test before release to customers, must be devised. Finally, if the model need not be of highest fidelity, the maintenance experts together with engineers will express their knowledge by formulating rules for component maintenance in an expert system. Interpretability of the data driven models created might show interesting patterns given the sensor inputs, i.e. engineers might gain insight to why certain types of failure occur. This is one of the major reasons of supporting interpretability at this stage. But this need not affect the performance of the model, instead model agnostic methods for interpretability should be preferred.

Once the predictive maintenance models have been put into production, they need to be evaluated and monitored in a smart way (the middle and right part of the figure). Typically, new models just put into production needs to be monitored more closely, compared to well-known models with known performance. But also these well-known models that seem to work well needs to be kept under surveillance. The question is how often and in what way to monitor the models, one obvious way is to create a feedback loop, one of the keys to becoming data driven. The feedback in this case should, ideally, contain a measure of how close to failure the component was and the prediction and confidence of the model. Here confidence is to be understood in the broad sense depending on the type of model we are dealing with. Given the type of component we are talking about, if it is replaced, as for example oil, belts etc. these can be analyzed to identify its remaining useful life, either directly by technicians or sent to experts. If the component involves interaction with the vehicle but do not render in objects which can be sent for analysis, one can use mediators or special instruments. These types of maintenance could for example be lubrication of parts, where a mechanic can do an ocular inspection and then report the assessment as feedback. In this case a picture could act as a mediator or we get a score could be given by the mechanic. An example of special instrument is the instrument used to measure the health status of batteries or an oil quality test equipment.

The best feedback loops should (1) be non-intrusive, (2) require no extra work effort and (3) should be transparent, i.e. the motive of the feedback loop should be clear for the organization, one motivation for this is to avoid the frustration that was common with drivers from the study by the ride-sharing companies presented earlier. The first two criteria's can be motivated from our short overview of the problems with NPM. If there is need for much paperwork or other manual processes or there is no easy way of measuring the outcome, one should consider abandoning this feedback loop, as it will not probably be successful over time.

These criterions can be for example applied to the battery health instrument used by the mechanics in the OEMs workshops today. This special instrument gives an answer to the batteries health status, and the mechanic needs to write the results into a (digital) work order report. It scores fairly high on point 3 above, but low on the other two points. If we updated the special instrument to work in alignment with the work order report (the feedback loop), where the value is feed into the work order report once the measurement is done, it would the score high on all three points, which is a situation to strive for. Due to the diversity of components needing predictions, feedback loops will have to be created in many creative ways to be able to evaluate and monitor the predictive models. The feedback loops serve two major roles, one is to verify that the models are valid, and also to adjust and refine the model as we gather more data. Both of these tasks can be automated and decision makers can put thresholds on alarms when human attention is needed, for example if models no longer can be considered valid.

As the cost for realizing feedback loops varies depending on different components, establishing a good feedback policy would require a cost analysis together with the already mentioned analysis of criticalness of component and hence model. Once such a base policy has been established, it dictates how often feedback is requested for a given component. The next question is how to best select which cases to sample? Random sampling is not a bad idea, but a fraction of the sampling can also be directed towards cases where the model is uncertain. This sampling policy would be mostly beneficial when the model is new and exposure to new cases are more frequent and needed. In general interpretability of models is not of big importance, instead other measures of model performance are needed, be it accuracy or the like. In special cases when the models no longer is valid or if experts need to understand the models for other reason, it would be sufficient to use model agnostic techniques to interpret the models.

The feedback loop could also change the transport service offer to become more dynamic, so given how and under which circumstances the customer utilize the transport service, the price is adjusted in real time.

5 Conclusions

It this paper a use-case has been investigated for a company that is in the transportation manufacturing industry which is an industry in transformation from only selling hardware to selling different levels of services together with the hardware. The focus has been on the maintenance program, how the program can become data driven, and the implications both on the organization and on the business. A framework has been proposed for facilitating the data driven business model w.r.t. aspects such as: Need for interpretability of models; How to create the necessary feedback loops; Which type of predictive models to use and when. In our framework we also try to draw lessons from what's been done earlier, like in the presented ride-sharing case and examples from NPM to avoid pitfalls which a data driven organization are facing. This framework will hopefully serve as an inspirational starting point for other organizations that are facing similar business challenges as the OEM.

References

1. Anderson, C., Brown, C.E.: The functions and dysfunctions of hierarchy. Res. Organ. Behav. **30**, 55–89 (2010)
2. Diefenbach, T.: New public management in public sector organizations: the dark sides of managerialistic enlightenment. Public Adm. **87**(4), 892–909 (2009)
3. Hammer, M.: The process audit. Harvard Bus. Rev. **85**, 111–119, 122 (2007)
4. Hoggett, P.: New modes of control in the public service. Public Adm. **74**(1), 9–32 (1996)
5. Karp, T.: Unpacking the mysteries of change: mental modelling. J. Change Manage. **5**(1), 87–96 (2005)
6. Lee, M.K., Kusbit, D., Metsky, E., Dabbish, L.: Working with machines: the impact of algorithmic and data-driven management on human workers. In: Proceedings of the 33rd Annual ACM Conference on Human Factors in Computing Systems, CHI 2015, pp. 1603–1612. ACM, New York (2015)
7. Lipton, Z.C.: The mythos of model interpretability. *CoRR,* abs/1606.03490 (2016)
8. Ribeiro, M.T., Singh, S., Guestrin, C.: "why should i trust you?": explaining the predictions of any classifier. In: Proceedings of the 22nd ACM SIGKDD International Conference on Knowledge Discovery and Data Mining, KDD 2016, pp. 1135–1144. ACM, New York (2016)
9. Shearer, C.: The CRISP-DM model: the new blueprint for data mining. J. Data Warehous. **5**(4), 13–22 (2000)
10. Srinivasan, V.: The Intelligent Enterprise in the Era of Big Data, 1st edn., Wiley (2017)
11. Tolomei, G., Silvestri, F., Haines, A., Lalmas, M.: Interpretable predictions of tree-based ensembles via actionable feature tweaking. In: Proceedings of the 23rd ACM SIGKDD International Conference on Knowledge Discovery and Data Mining, KDD 2017, pp. 465–474. ACM, New York (2017)

A Multi-factor Authentication Method for Security of Online Examinations

Abrar Ullah[1(✉)], Hannan Xiao[2], and Trevor Barker[2]

[1] School of Computing and Management, Cardiff Metropolitan University, Cardiff, UK
aaaullah@cardiffmet.ac.uk

[2] School of Computer Science, University of Hertfordshire, Hatfield, UK
{H.xiao,T.l.barker}@herts.ac.uk

Abstract. Security of online examinations is the key to success of remote online learning. However, it faces many conventional and non-conventional security threats. Impersonation and abetting are rising non-conventional security threats, when a student invites a third party to impersonate or abet in a remote exam. This work proposed dynamic profile questions authentication to identify that the person taking an online test is the same who completed the course work. This is combined with remote proctoring to prevent students from taking help from a third party during exam. This research simulated impersonation and abetting attacks in remote online course and laboratory based control simulation to analyse the impact of dynamic profile questions and proctoring. The study also evaluated effectiveness of the proposed method. The findings indicate that dynamic profile questions are highly effective. The security analysis shows that impersonation attack was not successful.

Keywords: Security · Authentication · Online examination

1 Introduction

Security is an important non-functional requirement for design and implementation of web-based applications. According to Schechter [1], it is a process of securing computer hardware, software, and networks against misuse and harm. A harm or misuse is a loss of desired system properties including confidentially, integrity and availability. The application of computer security has a wider scope, including hardware, software and network security. The focus of this research is application-level security, which falls into the information security context. Online summative assessment faces a number conventional and non-conventional security threats. The conventional threats include common web application threats. These are prevented and mitigated using the same approaches adopted for many web applications. However, the non-conventional threats are beyond the scope of many conventional security methods. These threats include collusion and impersonation during online assessments. This research proposes the use of dynamic profile questions and remote proctoring to prevent against impersonation and abetting in a remote online examination. This paper reports an empirical

A.-S. K. Pathan et al. (Eds.): SGIoT 2018, LNICST 256, pp. 131–138, 2019.

study using an online course and laboratory based session where participants simulated an impersonation and abetting attack in presence of a live proctor.

2 Background

Security is protection of assets. According to Ullah [2], asset is anything that has value for an organisation. Tajuddin [3] states that information security is protection of valuable "information". According to ISO/IEC 27002 [4], it is the protection of information from a wide range of threats that ensures business continuity and minimises business risks. The concept of business can be applied in any commercial or non-commercial context, such as online learning. The focus and research context of this work relates to summative assessment or remote online examinations. The growth in the use of online learning in higher education has been documented and reported in many studies [5–9]. It has attracted significant research focus on developing and delivering secure, efficient and effective learning environments. However, there have been many concerns about the security of online learning environments. With increasing demand, there are equally increasing concerns for the integrity of the summative assessment also known as online examinations [10].

The work is part of an ongoing research on security and usability of authentication by challenge questions. The authors conducted multiple empirical studies to analyse usability and security threats of text-based, image-based and dynamic profile questions to mitigate impersonation and abetting attacks [11, 12]. In these attacks, a student invites a third party to impersonate or abet in an online examination scenario. In the previous studies, the author proposed and evaluated a text-based challenge questions approach [13]. However, these questions were reported with usability and security issues [14]. In a similar vein, the use of image-based questions revealed improved usability [15], however, these questions were not sufficient to mitigate impersonation and abetting. In order to address the security issues, the authors proposed dynamic profile questions [7]. These questions are created in the background when a student performs learning activities. Individual student profile is built during the learning process. To access an online assessment, the student is presented with a subset of questions randomly extracted from his/her profile. In a recent study, the authors conducted a focus group study [6] with online programme tutors who recommended the use of dynamic profile questions [7], remote proctoring [16], and a secure browser to mitigate impersonation and abetting attacks.

The focus group study presented in an earlier study indicates that the use of dynamic profile questions with a secure browser and proctoring (ProctorU) [16] can positively influence collusion attacks. As described above, the dynamic profile questions are created non-intrusively and non-distractingly in the background when a student performs learning activities [7]. Using this method, a student's profile is built and consolidated in the background during the learning process. Students are not aware of which questions will be asked for authentication. This attempts to verify that the person who is taking the online test is the same individual who completed the coursework. The use of a secure browser and proctoring monitors an online examination, and attempts to ensure that a student is not taking help from the Internet or an abettor sitting close by or remotely. However, a student may still circumvent the system and share access credentials with an impersonator before the test session. Furthermore, usability attributes such as effectiveness is also important for secure implementation of authentication methods. The effectiveness is an important attribute defined by the International Organisation for Standards (ISO) which contributes to the usability [17]. In the context of this study, effectiveness means that students were able to answer dynamic profile questions correctly with a low error rate. This study will investigate the following:

- The effectiveness of dynamic profile questions in a proctored examination.
- Whether a student can share information about learning activities and experience with a third party impersonator using email, instant messaging, phone, or face-to-face meeting before an online test session, and how successful the impersonator is in answering the dynamic profile questions.

3 Research Methodology

This study was conducted using a real online course followed by a controlled laboratory-based simulation session. The usability test and risk-based security assessment methods were adopted to evaluate the usability and security of dynamic profile questions. The usability test method is a usability inspection, which tends to focus on the interaction between humans and computers [18]. Using this method, the representative users – i.e. students – work on typical system tasks on an online course and examination, which implements dynamic profile questions in a proctored test. In this study, the system tasks were simulated in a laboratory-based environment. The usability evaluation scale was used to translate the effectiveness analysis. This scale describes the usability of products in the 90 s as exceptional, 80 s as good, 70 s as acceptable, and anything below 70 indicates usability issues that are cause for concern [19].

The risk-based security assessment approach provides rapid quantification of security level risks associated with processes [20]. This method focuses on the test of features and functions of artefacts based on the risk of their failure using abuse case scenarios [21]. An abuse case scenario was simulated to investigate impersonation attacks, when dynamic profile questions are implemented for authentication of students in a proctored examination.

This study was conducted in a remote online learning environment and face-to-face sessions involving on-campus students. It was organised into two phases described below i.e. Phase I – online course and Phase II – abuse case simulation.

3.1 Phase I – Online Course and Student Pairing

In Phase I of the study, an online course was conducted to provide learning opportunities for students and facilitate the collusion abuse case scenario. The structure of Phase-I is described below.

- **PHP & MySQL Course Design:** A 'PHP and MySQL' online course was organised with three weekly modules, which included lessons, forum discussions, assignments, quizzes, grades and student reflection at the end of each week. The course was set up and deployed in the MOODLE Learning Management System (LMS) on a remote web server accessible on the Internet. Students were required to invest 10 h weekly learning effort for 15 days in a span of three weeks.
- **Participants Recruitment:** On-campus students from the School of Computer Science, University of Hertfordshire, were recruited to participate in the study and the online course. The course was advertised on the StudyNet. To motivate students the course was offered free of charge. Participants were selected on the basis that they knew each other already. They were also required to have basic programming knowledge in order to enrol. A total of 12 students were enrolled and completed the three-week course. There were 7 (58%) male and 5 (42%) female participants. They were also enrolled in BSc/MSc programmes which were helpful in setting up face-to-face meetings to present the study structure and research objectives, and perform the abuse case scenario in a laboratory.
- **Presentation and Students Registration:** Participants were required to attend a face-to-face 15 min presentation on the course structure and research objectives, before registration. They were also provided detailed information on an impersonation abuse case scenario. After the presentation, all participants signed the consent forms mandated by the University ethics regulations.
- **Pairing up of Participants for Impersonation:** In order to perform the impersonation, each participant was paired up with a fellow student (classmate), where both participants confirmed that they were familiar already. All participants consented to share learning experience and activities with their pairs. They were informed about the format of an impersonation abuse case scenario, which was conducted towards the end of the course.
- **Online Course Work:** The instructor-led course was conducted over a period of three weeks. Participants were required to submit their weekly assignments in order to access their weekly quizzes. Each assignment was based on the weekly course content, which ensured participants' engagement. It was mandatory for each participant to take their weekly quizzes and provide a 'reflection feedback' towards the end of each week.
- **Creating Dynamic Profile Questions:** Dynamic profile questions were created manually during the course for each individual student and stored in a Microsoft Word file in a secure location. These questions were created on a daily basis for each participant after access to course content including lessons, assignment submission, assignment grades, quiz completion, feedback and reflection, and forum discussion. This helped with creating and consolidating a profile for each participant. A total of 28 dynamic profile questions were created for each participant. Dynamic profile questions created during the coursework were not shown to any participant during the online course until the abuse case scenario described in the following section.

3.2 Phase II – Impersonation Abuse Case Scenario

This phase was performed towards the end of three week online course described in Phase I above. This study simulated the following impersonation abuse case scenario:

1. Participants were paired up before registration as described above in Phase I.
2. Dynamic profile questions for each participant were manually created and stored in their respective profiles. These questions were extracted from student activities on a daily basis, as described above in Phase I.
3. Participants were asked to share their learning experience, learning activities, and cues with their pairs during the course. They were allowed to share this information using any communication means, e.g. email, phone, WhatsApp, Skype, face-to-face meeting, Facebook, Facetime, SMS, printed paper, etc. They were required to memorise the shared information for simulating impersonation in a proctored examination.
4. At the end of week three, participants attended a laboratory-based simulation session.
5. Participants were informed about the format of simulating the laboratory-based proctored session. They were required to answer the questionnaire from memory and were not allowed to use an electronic or printed copy of the information shared by their pairs for impersonation. Also, they were not allowed to communicate or share information when answering the two questionnaires in the following order:
   (a) **Questionnaire 1 (Effectiveness)**: Participants were asked to answer paper-based Questionnaire 1 with a total of 10 dynamic profile questions randomly extracted from their own profiles created during the course work in Phase I.
   (b) **Questionnaire 2 (Impersonation)**: After answering Questionnaire 1, the participants were asked to answer a paper-based Questionnaire 2 with a total of 5 dynamic profile questions randomly extracted from their pair's profile to simulate impersonation.

4 Results

This section aims to evaluate the usability of dynamic profile questions in the presence of a live proctor. At the end of week three, 12 participants answered 120 dynamic profile questions which were created during the course. Results of the abuse case scenario is also analysed to determine the outcome of an impersonation attack.

4.1 Effectiveness

The effectiveness is considered to be the degree of accuracy of participants' responses. It is an important usability factor which indicates a degree of completeness with which users achieve a specified task in a certain context [22]. In the context of this study, it means that participants were able to provide correct answers to their dynamic profile questions correctly with a low error rate. It was analysed on the data collected from participants' answers on paper-based questionnaire 1 in a laboratory-based session.

Table 1 column 2 shows the mean of correct answers to dynamic profile questions in order to analyse effectiveness. The findings show 114 (95%) correct answers, which indicates positive outcome.

Table 1. Usability and security analysis

	Effectiveness	Impersonation
1	10 (100%)	2 (20%)
2	10 (100%)	1 (10%)
3	9 (90%)	3 (30%)
4	9 (90%)	3 (30%)
5	10 (100%)	2 (20%)
6	9 (90%)	1 (10%)
7	10 (100%)	2 (20%)
8	9 (90%)	2 (20%)
9	9 (90%)	3 (30%)
10	9 (90%)	2 (20%)
11	10 (100%)	2 (20%)
12	10 (100%)	3 (30%)
Total	114 (95%)	26 (22%)

According to the usability scale and letter grades (70%–79% acceptable, 80%–89% good, more than 90% exceptional) described by [17], 95% correct answers is an exceptional effectiveness.

4.2 Impersonation in Presence of Live Proctoring

The abuse case scenario was performed to decide if dynamic profile questions can mitigate impersonation in a proctored exam. In a laboratory-based session, participants answered paper-based Questionnaire 2 consisting of five dynamic profile questions on behalf of their pairs. They memorised the shared information during pairing and answered the questionnaire from memory. These questions implemented five multiple choice options and the probability of a correct answer to a random guessing would be 1/5th or 20%. In the impersonation abuse case scenario, participants answered 26 (22%) of the questions correctly on behalf of their pairs. These questions were not shown to any participant during the online course and presented at the final stage of the study to evaluate their ability to circumvent the dynamic profile question approach and impersonate students in the presence of a live proctor. The findings in Table 1 column 3 show that the sharing of information associated with individuals' learning experience led to correct answers just above 1/5th of the total questions.

To determine the significance of difference in the means of correct answers to dynamic profile questions by a student and a third party impersonator, a one-way ANOVA was performed on the data shown in Table 1 columns 2 and 3, which shows a significant difference $F = 596$; $p = 0.00$ $(p < 0.01)$; eta-squared □2 = 0.97..

An ANOVA test on a small sample size may not produce significant values due to insufficient power. However, findings of the test here yielded significant value.

In a practical situation, this may fail the authentication and alert the proctor or invigilator. This shows that students were able to answer their own challenge questions presented in the previous section; however, collusion between students and impersonators was not successful.

5 Conclusion

This study examined the use of dynamic profile questions in a proctored examination. Participants shared information using mobile phones, emails, chat, and face-to-face meetings at their own convenience before an online examination in pairs. They memorised the shared information and answered the questionnaire on dynamic profile questions on behalf of their pairs in the presence of a proctor. The results showed that dynamic profile questions decreases impersonation attacks when implemented with live proctoring. Participants' sharing helped the impersonators to provide 26 (22%) correct answers in the impersonation attack, which is just above 20%, which is the percentage of correct answers by chance. There was a significant difference ($p < 0.01$) in the correct answers between a student (114: 95%) and an impersonator (26: 22%). This indicates that, dynamic profile questions extracted from course content and submissions makes sharing harder for students and could be implemented for secure authentication. However, future work is warranted on a larger sample size.

References

1. Schechter, S.E.: Computer Security Strength & Risk: A Quantitative Approach. Harvard University Cambridge, Massachusetts, Massachusetts (2004)
2. Ullah, A.: Security and Usability of Authentication by Challenge Questions in Online Examination. University of Hertfordshire, Hatfield (2017)
3. Tajuddin, S., Olphert, W., Doherty, N.: Relationship between stakeholders' information value perception and information security behaviour. In: International Conference on Integrated Information (IC-ININFO 2014): Proceedings of the 4th International Conference on Integrated Information 2015. AIP Publishing (2015)
4. Sahibudin, S., Sharifi, M., Ayat, M.: Combining ITIL, COBIT and ISO/IEC 27002 in order to design a comprehensive IT framework in organizations. In: Modeling & Simulation, 2008 AICMS 2008 Second Asia International Conference on 2008. IEEE (2008)
5. Buzzetto-More, N.: Student perceptions of various e-learning components Interdisciplinary. J. E-Learn. Learn. Objects **4**(1), 113–135 (2008)
6. Ullah, A., Barker, T., Xiao, H.: A focus group study: usability and security of challenge question authentication in online examinations. In: International Conference on Information Technology and Applications (ICITA). Academic Alliance International, Sydney Australia (2017)
7. Ullah, A., Xiao, H., Barker, T.: A dynamic profile questions approach to mitigate impersonation in online examinations. J. Grid Comput. (Knowl. Discov.), 1–15 (2018)

8. Allen, I.E., Seaman, J.: Online Nation Five Years of Growth in Online learning Needham. Sloan Consortium, Mass (2007)
9. Koohang, A., Riley, L., Smith, T., Schreurs, J.: E-learning and constructivism: from theory to application Interdisciplinary. J. E-Learn. Learn. Objects **5**(1), 91–109 (2009)
10. Watson, G., Sottile, J.: Cheating in the digital age: do students cheat more in online courses? Online J. Distance Learn. Adm. **13**(1), n1 (2010)
11. Ullah, A., Xiao, H., Barker, T.: A dynamic profile questions approach to mitigate impersonation in online examinations. J. Grid Comput. 1–15 (2018)
12. Ullah, A., Xiao, H., Barker, T.: A study into the usability and security implications of text and image based challenge questions in the context of online examination. Educ. Inf. Technol. 1–27 (2018)
13. Ullah, A., Xiao, H., Lilley, M.: Profile based student authentication in online examination. In: International Conference on Information Society 2012. IEEE, London (2012)
14. Ullah, A., Xiao, H., Barker, T., Lilley, M.: Evaluating security and usability of profile based challenge questions authentication in online examinations. J. Internet Serv. Appl. **5**(1), 2 (2014)
15. Ullah, A., Xiao, H., Barker, T., Lilley, M.: Graphical and text based challenge questions for secure and usable authentication in online examinations. In: The 9th International Conference for Internet Technology and Secured Transactions (ICITST) 2014. IEEE, London (2014)
16. Mahmood, N.: Remote Proctoring Software Means Students Can Now Take Exams From Home. Technological News Portal; 2010 [cited 2011 13/07/2011]. http://thetechjournal.com/science/remote-proctoring-software-means-students-can-now-take-exams-from-home.xhtml
17. Iso9241-11. Ergonomic Requirements for Office Work with Visual Dispaly Terminals, Part 11: Guidance on Usability. ISO 9241-11. Geneva1998)
18. Corry, M.D., Frick, T.W., Hansen, L.: User-centered design and usability testing of a web site: an illustrative case study. Educ. Technol. Res. Dev. **45**(4), 65–76 (1997)
19. Bangor, A., Kortum, P., Miller, J.: Determining what individual SUS scores mean: adding an adjective rating scale. J. Usability Stud. **4**(3), 114–123 (2009)
20. Ni, M., Mccalley, J.D., Vittal, V., Tayyib, T.: Online risk-based security assessment. IEEE Trans. Power Syst. **18**(1), 258–265 (2003)
21. Mcgraw, G.: Software security & privacy. IEEE **2**(2), 80–83 (2004)
22. Seffah, A., Kececi, N., Donyaee, M.: QUIM: a framework for quantifying usability metrics in software quality models. In: Quality Software, 2001 Proceedings Second Asia-Pacific Conference on 2001. IEEE (2001)

Evaluation Metrics for Big Data Project Management

Munir Ahmad Saeed and Mohiuddin Ahmed(✉)

Canberra Institute of Technology, Canberra, Australia
saeed.munir@cit.edu.au, m.ahmed.au@ieee.org

Abstract. In this paper, we investigated the current scenario of big data project management followed by success criteria. Our research found that, the evaluation metrics are generic and no universal metric available for the big data projects. Therefore, we have proposed few evaluation metrics suitable for big data projects.

Keywords: Big data · Project management · Evaluation metrics

1 Introduction

Though project management started in late 1950 but project success started attracting the imagination of researchers as project management matured in to an independent discipline since 1980s. Success is a subjective in nature and it may mean different to different people. However, project management professionals and researchers commonly identified project success evaluation metrics as completing a project within triple constraints such as at cost, time and within specifications. With the passage of time various other metrics were added to the wish list and most recently projects benefits realization has been included as key evaluation metrics for project success. Big data projects are inherently software projects and according to Standish Report 2017, the project success in software development is abysmally low. Big data projects are struggling to convince top managements of large organizations for the value of resources spent on such projects. Therefore it is pertinent to identify evaluation metrics for big data projects success. This paper discusses the current state of big data projects and challenges faced with regard to success and how to measure success of big data projects. It also identifies metrics for the evaluation of the success of big data projects.

The rest of the paper is organized as follows. Section 2 discusses big data project management. Section 3 defines success in big data projects and Sect. 4 outlines the evaluation criteria for such projects followed by the proposed metrics. Section 5 concludes the paper.

A.-S. K. Pathan et al. (Eds.): SGIoT 2018, LNICST 256, pp. 139–142, 2019.
https://doi.org/10.1007/978-3-030-05928-6_14

2 Big Data Project Management

The CHAOS report 2017 by the Standish Group points out that nearly $250 Billion were invested on IT applications projects in the US alone but the success rate has been far less than desirable and only 28% of software projects at small size companies were completed on time and cost. Which means rest of the projects were either cancelled (31%) or massively (53%)will be over budget by one hundred-ninety times. The report further states that in the US medium size organizations fared well with 16% project success rate, whereas larger corporations had an abysmal 9% project success rate. However, the report did not explain whether the organization size has role to play in project success. Big data projects being inherently software applications project are expected to suffer from similar challenges experienced by mainstream IT applications projects. As according to Informatica (a reputed software development company), even the data analytics proof of concepts, being small projects, fail to complete on time and budget and subsequently these projects were unsuccessful in meeting top management expectations. Big data projects need to convince the top management of the utility of projects and currently in companies, where such projects are being implemented only 27% executives consider their data projects are successful because there are only 13% companies where big data projects are in full scale production. It is found that for project success and subsequent organizational change, top management support (TSM) is one of the most important critical success factors. Young and Poon [1] argue that TMS is more critical for project success than other traditional success factors.

Though the mainstream project management is yet to give due attention to big data projects. Since big data projects are less known, therefore there is a need for research to identify the factors behind the success/failure. However, Informatica has identified some of the factors that contribute to the failure of big data proof of concepts such as projects failing to align with the strategic objectives of sponsoring executives, lack of planning and design, scope creep and ignoring data management. According to Informatica, if projects align to top management's strategic plans, it guarantees whole hearted support of organization executives. In order for projects to ensure executives' support, the projects must align to the organization strategic objectives by creating value to the organization.

3 Success in Project Management

Traditional project management literature identifies the triple constraint or the Iron Triangle of cost, time and specifications as project success criteria [2]. However, as the project management became more popular tool for achieving organizational strategic tool, the success criteria also added various other variables. It is argued that trade literature identifies schedule, budget and customer satisfaction, as the measures of project success. Time and budget are already known components of iron triangle of project success; however, the customer satisfaction has been identified equally important project success measure later on [3].

Pinto and Slevin [4] identified 10 project success factors such as project mission, top management support, project schedule plan, client consultation, personnel matters such as human resources and training, technical tasks - adequate technology to support project, client acceptance, monitoring and feedback, communication and troubleshooting. Though the research on project success was in rudimentary form when these success factors were identified by Pinto and Slevin [4], however, these factors echo in the current research as well. The recent research puts emphasis on client satisfaction in addition to traditional success factors such as time, cost and specifications. Similarly, Freeman and Beale [5] identified seven main elements of project success criteria and state that first five have been more frequently mentioned:

- Technical performance
- Efficiency of execution
- Managerial and organizational implications (mainly customer satisfaction)
- Personal growth
- Manufacturability and business performance
- Technical innovation

4 Big Data Projects Evaluation Criteria

On the basis of the above brief discussion on project success following variables can be employed as the basis of the evaluation of the project success.

- Alignment to organizational strategic objectives
- A strong business case leading to approval of projects proof of concept on merit
- Project benefits realization
- Completion of project on time, cost and specifications
- Quantifiable objectives based on SMART methodology
- Technical performance of the big data application
- Technical innovation
- Top management support (ownership)
- Employment of project management methodology along with software development life cycle processes
- Continuous interest of top management through governance and political support
- Stability of organizational strategic objectives to ensure continuous support to ongoing projects

4.1 Proposed Metrics for Application Specific Big Data Projects

Based on the above discussion, we are encouraged to propose a number of evaluation metrics for big data projects as below:

- The efficiency of the application to achieve its objectives such as change in business processes and effective decision making

- Appropriate technology
- Completion on time, cost and required scope of functions and features
- Effective scope definition and scope change management as Big Data Projects fail 30% more than IT Project, due to poorly defined scope and uncontrolled scope changes
- Effective Risk and quality management against poor decision making and quality
- Organizational learning and changes as a result of big data applications
- Contributing towards the achievement of strategic objectives through benefits realization
- Effective change management of processes as a result of big data application

5 Conclusions

Project success is an old and continuous debate in the mainstream project management literature. Initially the success criteria was based on the iron triangles of on time, on cost and as per specifications, but later various other variables such as customer satisfaction, technical performance and quite recently the realization of promised business benefits have been added to the project success criteria. Big data projects, though different from IT applications, suffer from similar challenges, such as poorly defined scope, scope creep, lack of clarity on project objectives leading to failure to provide business value. In addition to the application a suitable project management methodology thus ensuring properly defined scope, effective scope change management, big data projects need to give due attention to benefits realization, which means giving more attention to project outcomes rather than outputs. For this to happen big data projects should be managed through Project Management Office (PMO) so that once the project is complete, it must ensure that promised organizational learning and value are harvested to the optimum levels.

References

1. Raymond, Y., Simon, P.: Top management support-almost always necessary and sometimes sufficient for success: findings from a fuzzy set analysis. Int. J. Proj. Manage. **31**(7), 943–957 (2013)
2. Atkinson, R.: Project management: cost, time and quality, two best guesses and a phenomenon, its time to accept other success criteria. Int. J. Proj. Manage. **17**(6), 337–342 (1999)
3. Dragon, M., Peerasit, P.: Standardized project management may increase development projects success. Int. J. Proj. Manage. **23**(3), 181–192 (2005)
4. Pinto, J.K., Slevin, D.P.: Critical success factors across the project life cycle: definitions and measurement techniques. Proj. Manage. J. **19**(3), 67–75 (1988)
5. Freeman, M., Beale, P.: Measuring project success. Proj. Manage. J. **23**(1), 8–17 (1992)

Author Index

Printed in the United States
By Bookmasters

Printed in the United States
By Bookmasters